STEER

A REAL-WORLD GUIDE TO CAREER CLARITY AND CHANGE

DR. ASHHAR AHMED SHAIKH

Made with ♥ on the Notion Press Platform
www.notionpress.com

Dedication

To the students and young professionals seeking clarity in an increasingly complex world, may this guide serve as a compass in your journey toward purposeful work and informed decisions.

To the educators, mentors, and parents who dedicate themselves to nurturing potential, your role in shaping future generations is both vital and invaluable.

This book is written in recognition of your aspirations, your challenges, and the transformative power of direction.

With sincere respect and commitment to your growth.

Contents

Contents

FOREWORD

We are living through one of the most transformative periods in human history. Technology is advancing at an unprecedented pace, industries are being reshaped overnight, and the definition of "a stable career" is constantly evolving. Amidst this whirlwind, today's youth face a paradox: endless possibilities, yet overwhelming uncertainty.

In this environment, one thing becomes clear—clarity is power.

Unfortunately, clarity is what many young individuals lack. While academic institutions equip students with knowledge, they often fall short in offering guidance for the real world. Career decisions—arguably among the most important in a person's life—are frequently made with limited information, little reflection, and immense pressure. That is what makes Steer: A Real-World Guide to Career Clarity and Change so essential. This book does more than simply outline job roles or recommend career tips. It provides a framework for thinking about careers in a modern, agile, and deeply personal way. It bridges the gap between aspiration and action, blending self-assessment tools, real-world insights, and practical roadmaps across industries—from technology to healthcare, creative fields to public service. It recognizes that no two journeys are the same, and that success is not a fixed destination but a path shaped by curiosity, growth, and adaptability.

What sets this work apart is its comprehensiveness and empathy. It speaks not only to students, but also to the educators, parents, and policy makers who are part of the larger ecosystem of guidance. It challenges outdated systems, advocates for career education as a lifelong process, and encourages its readers to steer—not drift—through the choices ahead.

Whether you're just beginning to explore your interests, making a pivot, or supporting someone else's path, this book offers the clarity, tools, and direction that our times demand. I commend the author for bringing such a timely and visionary guide into the world. Steer will no doubt become an indispensable companion for those navigating the journey from confusion to conviction in their careers.

Preface

In an age marked by rapid technological advancement and overwhelming choice, today's youth stand at a confusing crossroads—rich in opportunity, yet paralyzed by uncertainty. While access to information has never been easier, clarity about one's purpose and career direction has never been more elusive. I have written Steer: A Real-World Guide to Career Clarity and Change to address this growing gap between potential and purposeful action.

This book is born out of years of observation, conversation, and collaboration with students, educators, parents, and professionals across industries. I've seen firsthand how the lack of structured career guidance can lead to aimlessness, anxiety, and wasted years. I've also witnessed the transformative power of clarity—when young people discover their direction, align their strengths, and step forward with intention.

Steer is not just a guidebook. It is a call to action. It is a practical roadmap for students, teachers, and institutions to reimagine career development in the 21st century. From demystifying industries and job roles to providing tools for self-discovery and strategic goal-setting, this book is designed to empower readers to make informed, confident, and adaptable career choices.

Whether you're a student standing at the threshold of decision, a teacher hoping to make your guidance more relevant, or a parent seeking to support without controlling, this book is for you. My hope is that it becomes not only a resource but also a companion as you navigate the lifelong journey of meaningful work and self-fulfillment.

- Dr. Ashhar Ahmed Shaikh

Acknowledgements

Writing Steer: A Real-World Guide to Career Clarity and Change has been a deeply personal and transformative journey. It would not have been possible without the support, insight, and encouragement of many individuals and communities who shaped both the book and the purpose behind it. First, I express my heartfelt gratitude to the students who inspired this work. Your questions, challenges, dreams, and determination gave this book its voice. Thank you for trusting me with your stories and for reminding me why this work matters. To the educators and mentors who go beyond the curriculum to guide young minds—thank you. Your dedication to empowering students to think critically about their future has been a constant source of motivation. To the professionals and industry leaders who generously shared their time, experiences, and perspectives—your input brought real-world depth and authenticity to this project. To my family and friends—thank you for your unwavering belief in me. Your patience and encouragement sustained me through every late night and early morning of writing, editing, and refining. To the researchers, writers, and thought leaders in education, career development, and youth empowerment—your work laid the foundation upon which this book stands.

Finally, to every young person trying to find their path: this book is for you. May it offer direction, confidence, and hope as you carve out a life of purpose and possibility.

With deepest gratitude,

- Dr. Ashhar Ahmed Shaikh

Prologue

This is not a book of rigid prescriptions. It is a guide, a mirror, and a map. It weaves together research, real-world roadmaps, reflective tools, and inspiring stories to help you explore, decide, and act. Whether you are a student, a parent, a teacher, or someone considering a change, Steer invites you to rethink what it means to build a career—and how to do it with clarity and courage.

Welcome to a journey of self-discovery, skill-building, and future-readiness. It's time to steer your course.

Contact Dr. Ashhar Ahmed Shaikh:

Email: ashhar@skillshark.in

LinkedIn: https://www.linkedin.com/in/ashharahmed/

Instagram: https://www.instagram.com/ashharahmedshaikh/

Contact: +91-9028095540

I

The Crisis of Career Clarity

More dangerous than unemployment is unemployability.

The Reality Today

Youth across the globe are under unprecedented pressure to "figure it out" early in life—what to study, where to work, and what they want to become. Yet, most are navigating this journey with:

- Outdated parental advice
- Peer pressure
- Misleading social media hype
- Academic systems designed for the 20th century

Despite being "digital natives," most youth lack career navigation tools and are stuck in reactive decision-making.

The Real Problem: A Triple Threat

Lack of Self-Understanding

Many students don't know:

- What they're good at
- What excites them
- What environment do they thrive in

Information Overload

Thousands of career options exist today—from ethical hacking to drone piloting to NFT art. With too many choices and no structured exposure, decision paralysis sets in.

A System Focused on Degrees, Not Direction

Education often focuses more on marks than mastery, forcing students into career tracks with little room for exploration.

The Impact of This Crisis

- Dropouts and Switchovers: Students changing courses or leaving education due to misaligned career choices.
- Anxiety and Burnout: When one's career feels forced or meaningless, mental health suffers.
- Stagnation: A talent mismatch leads to low productivity and wasted potential.

What the Data Shows

- According to a LinkedIn report, 70% of professionals feel they chose the wrong career in their early years.
- In India alone, 93% of engineering graduates are not employable in core engineering roles, as per a 2022 study by Aspiring Minds.

- Globally, 42% of Gen Z consider mental health as a major barrier to achieving their career goals (Deloitte Millennial Survey 2021).
- 93% of students (aged 14–21) in India are aware of only 7 career options, despite 250+ roles being available. *(Mindler-CII Survey)*

But There's a Silver Lining

Clarity is not given; it is built. With the right framework, exposure, and tools, young people can chart fulfilling career paths. That's what this book is here to help with.

What's Ahead in This Book?

This book is not just theory. It's a step-by-step guide to help you:

- Understand yourself better
- Learn where the world is going
- Choose a career path with confidence & Develop the skills needed
- Use tools and platforms that matter
- Craft a realistic, actionable roadmap

End-of-Chapter Exercise

Quick Reflection
Write down your answers to the following:

- What career did you dream of as a child?
- Who are your current role models and why?
- What are you currently doing to explore career options?

Mini Assignment

Ask 3 people in different professions & document your findings.:

- "What do you do, and how did you choose your career?"
- "What would you do differently if you had to start again?"

II

Knowing Yourself – The Foundation of Career Success

Before you choose a path, you must first understand the traveler.

Why Self-Discovery Is the First Step

Career choices are often made based on external factors: marks, money, market trends, or family expectations. But a fulfilling career—one that offers purpose, passion, and progress—starts with internal clarity. Choosing your career without knowing yourself is like setting sail without a compass. This chapter is about that compass.

What is Self-Awareness?

Self-awareness is the conscious knowledge of your own:

- Strengths and weaknesses
- Interests and passions
- Values and motivators
- Personality traits
- Workstyle preferences

It is the foundation for:

- Making decisions with confidence
- Choosing roles aligned with your energy
- Avoiding burnout or boredom
- Communicating effectively in interviews and teams

Tools for Self-Discovery

1. SWOT Analysis: Strengths, Weaknesses, Opportunities, Threats

- Strengths: What do you naturally do well? (Skills, traits, knowledge)
- Weaknesses: Where do you struggle or lack interest?
- Opportunities: What trends, tools, or chances can you use to grow?
- Threats: What external risks could slow you down?

Fill out your personal SWOT with examples like:

- Strength: Good public speaking
- Weakness: Poor at data analysis
- Opportunity: Growing podcasting market
- Threat: Parental pressure to choose engineering

2. MBTI – 16 Personalities

The Myers-Briggs Type Indicator (MBTI) assessment is a tool that helps people increase their self-awareness, understand, and appreciate differences in others. The MBTI–16 Personalities will help you understand how you process the world and make decisions. Sample Types:

- INTJ: The Architect – Strategic and logical
- ENFP: The Campaigner – Creative and outgoing
- ISTJ: The Logistician – Responsible and organized

Use your results to assess:

- Ideal work environments
- Type of communication styles
- Preferred industries or team roles

3. Ikigai – Finding Your Reason for Being

A Japanese framework combining:

- What you love
- What are you good at
- What the world needs
- What can you be paid for

Make a 4-circle Venn diagram. Brainstorm each circle. Look for intersections! Example:

- Love: Writing
- Good at: Storytelling
- The world needs: Awareness of sustainability
- Paid for: Content creation for green startups

Ikigai = Green communication strategist

4. Holland Code (RIASEC)

Helps map careers to interest areas:

- Realistic – Doers (e.g., engineers, mechanics)
- Investigative – Thinkers (e.g., scientists, analysts)
- Artistic – Creators (e.g., designers, writers)
- Social – Helpers (e.g., teachers, therapists)
- Enterprising – Persuaders (e.g., marketers, leaders)
- Conventional – Organizers (e.g., accountants, managers)

Use a free test (like at truity.com) to get your top 3 types and matched career suggestions.

Self-Reflection Questions

Ask yourself:

- What activities make me lose track of time?
- When do I feel most energized?
- What have people consistently praised me for?
- What tasks do I avoid or procrastinate?
- What values do I refuse to compromise?

Case Study – Aarav's Story

- Background: Aarav was a top scorer expected to become an engineer.
- Problem: He hated physics and found coding dry. He loved organizing school events.
- Action: After doing MBTI and Ikigai, he realized he enjoyed people interaction and planning.
- Now: He's pursuing Event Management and interning with a wedding planning startup. His parents saw his growth and now fully support his career choice.

Moral: When your career aligns with your personality, growth feels natural.

End-of-Chapter Activities

1. Complete Your Career Compass Pack

- SWOT Analysis
- MBTI or RIASEC result
- Ikigai circles
- Top 5 values (use a list from resources like VIA Character Strengths)

2. Write Your Career Story (So Far) in 1 page:

- What career ideas have you considered?
- What influenced those choices?
- What new clarity do you now have about yourself?

III

The Career Clarity Framework – The STEER Model

Clarity doesn't come from thinking more. It comes from structured reflection, exposure, and action.

You wouldn't build a house without a blueprint.
You wouldn't drive to a new city without a map.
Then why build a life or career without a proven process?

This chapter introduces the STEER Model—a five-step, repeatable framework designed to help anyone (especially youth) navigate from confusion to clarity in career decisions.

The STEER Model Overview

S – Self-Awareness
T – Trends & Industry Exposure
E – Exploration & Experimentation
E – Execution (Skill-Building & Action Plan)
R – Realignment & Reflection

Let's break down each component in detail.

S – Self-Awareness (Who am I?)

- Personality types
- Interests and passions
- Core values
- Natural abilities and talents

Goal: Build a strong identity before choosing a path.

T – Trends & Industry Exposure (Where is the world going?)
Don't pick a career based only on what's popular today—pick based on where the world is headed.

Key Concepts:

- Understanding macro trends (AI, sustainability, remote work, EVs, creator economy)
- Learning about emerging and evolving careers
- Mapping your interests to future industries

Activities:

- Read reports (e.g., WEF Future of Jobs, McKinsey skills reports)
- Watch interviews of professionals in new-age roles (YouTube, podcasts)
- Attend webinars, expos, and startup events

Examples of Trending Careers:

- AI & Automation - Prompt Engineer, ML Ops Expert
- Environment - Climate Analyst, Carbon Auditor
- Web3 & Blockchain - Token Economist, NFT Strategist
- Education Tech - Instructional Designer, Learning Engineer
- Health & Wellness - Wellness Coach, Healthtech Developer
- Cybersecurity - Ethical Hacker, Privacy Analyst

E – Exploration & Experimentation (What feels right?)

Exposure changes everything. You can't choose what you've never experienced.

Methods of Exploration:

- Shadowing professionals – Spend a day with someone in your dream job
- Internships – Try small stints in startups, NGOs, or corporate projects
- Freelancing – Use platforms like Fiverr, Upwork, and Internshala
- Hackathons / Bootcamps – Fast-track exposure to industries like design, coding, etc.
- Volunteering – Gain experience and test if your values align

Framework: Try-Test-Tweak

- Try a short experience
- Test how it feels and what you learned
- Tweak your understanding and next action

E – Execution (How do I make it real?)

Without action, even the best plans mean nothing. This is where planning, upskilling, and personal branding come in.

Sub-Steps:

1. Build Skills (Hard + Soft)

- Learn from platforms: SkillShark, Coursera, Udemy, Khan Academy
- Do mini-projects
- Improve communication, emotional intelligence, and teamwork

2. Craft a Learning Plan

Tool: T-L-P Grid

- Tools to learn
- Level to reach (Beginner, Intermediate, Advanced)
- Platform (where to learn)

Skill - Tool - Level - Platform

- Data Analysis - Excel - Intermediate - LinkedIn Learning
- Public Speaking - Toastmasters - Advanced - Practice groups
- Digital Marketing - Google Ads - Beginner - Google Skillshop

3. Build Your Portfolio

- Document projects on GitHub, Behance, Medium
- Make a video resume
- Start a blog or YouTube channel on your journey

4. Network Intentionally

- LinkedIn outreach
- Career-specific Discord servers, Reddit, forums
- Attend offline meetups

R – Realign & Reflect (Is it working?)
You're allowed to change direction—just don't stop moving.
Every few months, pause and reflect:

- Am I still excited about this?
- What am I struggling with?
- Do I need to pivot or persist?

Tools:

- Monthly Reflection
- Career Scorecard (0–10 rating on fulfillment, learning, impact)
- Feedback from mentors, managers, or peers

A Full STEER Example: Ananya's Story

Ananya, a commerce student, was confused about her path.
    S: She found she loved organizing and was an extrovert (MBTI: ENFJ)
    T: She explored Event Management and EdTech trends
    E: Interned with a startup that did college events
    E: Took online courses, built a portfolio, and networked
    R: Realized she enjoyed training more than logistics

She pivoted from Event Manager to Career Coach for youth

End-of-Chapter Activity

Fill in your current understanding:

Self: _______________________

Trends I'm watching: _______________________

Exploration plans: _______________________

Skill-building plan: _______________________

Reflection cycle: _______________________

IV
Career Landscapes – Understanding Industries, Functions, and Roles

You can't find the right seat if you don't understand how the bus is laid out.

This chapter helps you navigate the professional world—breaking it down into industries, functions, and roles, so you can see how your career can take shape across sectors.

What Is a Career Landscape?

Think of the career world like a huge city:

- Industries are the neighborhoods (e.g., Healthcare, Tech, Finance).
- Functions are the types of jobs people do (e.g., Marketing, Engineering).
- Roles are the specific seats (e.g., Digital Marketer, Front-End Developer).

Why This Matters:

Most students and professionals only know the few jobs they see around them—doctor, engineer, teacher, manager. But in reality, every industry is filled with hundreds of unique roles that match different interests and skillsets.

Understanding Industries

1. Technology & Innovation

- Examples: Software, AI, Cybersecurity, Robotics, Web3, Gaming
- Key Players: Google, Microsoft, Infosys, NVIDIA, OpenAI
- Typical Roles: Software Engineer, UI/UX Designer, Data Analyst, ML Engineer
- Who It Suits: Problem-solvers, tinkerers, coders, digital creatives

2. Healthcare & Biotech

- Examples: Hospitals, Pharma, MedTech, Wellness Startups
- Key Players: Pfizer, Medtronic, Apollo Hospitals, Practo
- Typical Roles: Doctor, Clinical Researcher, Medical Sales Rep, Biotech Analyst
- Who It Suits: People-oriented, research-loving, detail-focused individuals

3. Finance & Business Services

- Examples: Banks, Fintech, Consulting, Accounting, VC firms
- Key Players: Goldman Sachs, Deloitte, Zerodha, Bain
- Typical Roles: Investment Banker, Financial Analyst, Consultant, CA, VC Associate
- Who It Suits: Analytical thinkers, number crunchers, deal-makers

4. Manufacturing & Core Engineering

- Examples: Automotive, Aerospace, Electronics, Energy
- Key Players: Tata Motors, Siemens, Tesla, GE
- Typical Roles: Mechanical Engineer, Production Supervisor, R&D Engineer, EV Designer
- Who It Suits: Hands-on builders, system thinkers, innovators

5. Education & Skill Development

- Examples: EdTech, K-12, Higher Education, Online Learning
- Key Players: Byju's, Unacademy, Teach for India, Khan Academy
- Typical Roles: Instructional Designer, Learning Experience (LX) Designer, Career Coach, Academic Researcher
- Who It Suits: Communicators, educators, trainers, and purpose-driven individuals

6. Media, Design & Content

- Examples: Film, Journalism, Animation, UI/UX, Content Creation
- Key Players: Netflix, Canva, Adobe, Vice Media, Instagram Creators
- Typical Roles: Content Strategist, Visual Designer, Copywriter, Video Editor
- Who It Suits: Creative thinkers, storytellers, designers, visual artists

7. Public Sector & Development

- Examples: Government, NGOs, Policy Think-Tanks, International Orgs
- Key Players: NITI Aayog, UNDP, Gates Foundation
- Typical Roles: Policy Analyst, Development Officer, Social Entrepreneur
- Who It Suits: Idealists, system changers, people who want impact

Understanding Functions

In the world of careers, a function refers to the type of work you do, regardless of the industry you're in. Think of it as your core skill area or job category—for example, whether you're designing, analyzing, selling, coding, or managing people. These functions remain mostly the same across industries, but how they're applied may differ. For instance, Marketing in the technology sector might focus on digital campaigns and SEO, while marketing in healthcare could involve awareness programs and field campaigns. The skills overlap, but the content and context change.

Here are some common functions:

- Engineering involves building things—software, machines, systems. It suits people who enjoy technical challenges, coding, and innovation.
- Marketing is about communicating value and building brand presence. It's great for creative thinkers, storytellers, and those who enjoy audience psychology.
- Sales revolves around convincing customers and driving revenue. It fits well with confident communicators who enjoy results-driven environments.
- Operations is about ensuring everything runs smoothly, whether it's a factory floor or a tech product rollout. This suits organizers, planners, and efficiency enthusiasts.
- Finance involves managing money, investments, and risk. Ideal for analytical minds and those comfortable with numbers.
- Human Resources (HR) focuses on people—recruiting, developing, and retaining talent. Empathetic, people-first individuals often thrive here.
- Product Management is a cross-functional role combining business, tech, and user experience. It's for strategic thinkers who enjoy overseeing the development of solutions.
- Design & UX focuses on making products useful, beautiful, and user-friendly. Creative individuals with a strong aesthetic sense fit well here.
- Research & Analysis is about gathering data and uncovering insights to guide decisions. If you love deep thinking and problem-solving, this might be for you.

- Customer Success & Support ensures customers are happy and supported after buying a product or service. It suits empathetic, service-oriented personalities.

Understanding which function aligns with your strengths and interests is essential for career clarity. You can work in your preferred industry in multiple capacities by choosing the right function—whether as a tech-savvy engineer, a marketing genius, a thoughtful researcher, or an empathetic HR manager.

Understanding Roles – The Specific Seat You Choose

Once you've figured out which industry and function you're interested in, the next step is identifying your role—the actual job title or position you would hold within a company.

Think of it like this:

- The industry is the field (e.g., EdTech, Automotive, Finance).
- The function is the type of work you want to do (e.g., Engineering, Marketing, Product).
- The role is the specific job you take on (e.g., UX Designer, Battery Engineer, Equity Analyst).

Each role is a combination of skills, responsibilities, and outputs tailored to that job. For example:

- In the EdTech industry, someone working in the design function could have the role of UX Designer.
- In the Automotive industry, someone in engineering could be a Battery Systems Engineer.
- In Finance, someone in analysis might be an Equity Research Analyst.
- In Public Policy, someone in strategy might be a Policy Consultant.
- In Gaming, someone in product management might become a Game Product Manager.

Your role is where your interests, skills, and personality converge. It's the most concrete part of your career path—it defines what you'll do every day, what you'll learn, and how you'll grow.

Key Insight: You don't have to commit to one role forever. As your skills and interests evolve, your roles can change too—within the same function or across different ones.

Career Misconceptions to Break – Clearing the Fog

One of the biggest obstacles to career clarity isn't lack of information—it's misinformation. Many students and professionals base their career decisions on myths, half-truths, or outdated advice. Let's break down some of the most common misconceptions that often derail people from finding meaningful and fulfilling work.

1. "I need to figure out my entire life at once."
   Many young people feel pressured to decide their entire future at 18 or 21. But the truth is, careers evolve. You'll likely shift roles, functions, or even industries multiple times. Focus instead on taking the next best step—a direction that aligns with your interests and strengths right now.

2. "There are only a few 'respectable' careers."
   This is a deeply rooted societal myth—often centered around becoming a doctor, engineer, or government officer. In reality, there are hundreds of valuable, impactful roles today—from data scientists and climate consultants to game developers and fintech entrepreneurs. Respect doesn't come from the job title—it comes from the excellence and authenticity you bring to it.

3. "Passion alone will lead me to success."
   While passion is important, it needs to be paired with skill-building, market relevance, and real-world experience. You might be passionate about music, but success comes from learning, practicing, and adapting to industry demands. Passion is the spark—discipline and direction are the fuel.

4. "Money is the only measure of success."
   Chasing high-paying jobs without considering your strengths or interests often leads to burnout. True career success is multi-dimensional: it includes

growth, fulfillment, health, impact, and yes, financial security—but not at the cost of everything else.

5. "The first job defines my whole career."

Many believe that their first job is a lifelong stamp—but it's not. It's just a starting point. What matters more is how you learn, network, and evolve over time. Many successful people took winding paths to get where they are.

6. "If I fail early, I'm not cut out for success."

Early failure is common—and often essential. Every industry leader has faced rejection, setbacks, or dead-ends. What matters is your ability to learn, reflect, and try again smarter. Failure is not the opposite of success—it's part of it.

7. "There's a 'perfect' career out there for me."

This belief can lead to endless searching and disappointment. Instead of chasing perfection, focus on alignment—where your skills, values, and interests meet a real-world opportunity. A great career is not found; it's built step-by-step.

8. "I must wait for the 'right opportunity' to act."

Waiting often turns into years of inaction. There's never a perfect time—what you need is movement. Start small, experiment, volunteer, take internships, or start side projects. Action creates clarity.

Mapping Your Options: A 3-Step Exercise

Step 1: Pick 3 Industries that excite you (e.g., Sustainability, Fintech, EdTech)

Step 2: Pick 2–3 Functions you might enjoy (e.g., Product Management, Marketing, Research)

Step 3: List at least 5 roles you want to explore

Examples:

EdTech → Product Management → Associate PM at SkillShark

Fintech → Research → Crypto Analyst at CoinDCX

Sustainability → Marketing → Climate Awareness Campaign Lead

End-of-Chapter Activity

Industry Exposure Tracker (List all the interested industries)

- Industry Name
- What excites me?
- Who do I follow?
- Resources I'll explore

Function Deep Dive

- What skills do I already have?
- What do I need to learn?

Role Reality Check

- Interview someone in the role OR watch 3 YouTube interviews of professionals in your chosen function.

V

Career Roadmaps – From Confusion to Clarity

"It's not the path that defines your future—it's how intentionally you walk it."

We live in an age where choices are abundant but direction is rare. Ask a young adult today what career they want, and you're likely to hear one of three answers:

- "I'm not sure."
- "Something in tech/business/design maybe?"
- Or worse, "Whatever pays well."

The confusion isn't due to a lack of ambition—it's the absence of structured guidance. Students and early professionals are often left to figure out their future by trial and error. While exploration is important, wandering without a map wastes time, energy, and usually, self-confidence. That's where Career Roadmaps come in. A career roadmap is a structured, step-by-step guide that helps you move from where you are to where you want to be.

It's a blend of:

- Who you are (your interests, strengths, and values),
- Where you're starting from, and
- What roles and industries align with your goals?

Why Career Roadmaps Matter

Imagine trying to build a house without a blueprint. You might know what you want—a two-story building with lots of sunlight and a big kitchen—but without a plan, your materials get wasted and progress stalls. Careers are no different.

- A clear roadmap helps you:
- Visualize your journey from student to professional.
- Set practical goals at each stage.
- Track progress and adjust direction as needed.
- Avoid burnout from constant guesswork and comparison.

Role-Based Career Mapping: A Better Way to Navigate

One of the most effective ways to create a roadmap is by starting with a role—the specific job or position you aspire to—and then mapping backward.

For example:

- If you want to become a Data Scientist, what should you study? What internships should you look for? What tools should you master?
- If your dream is to be a Product Manager in Gaming, what kind of portfolio would help? What kind of companies hire juniors into such roles?
- If you aim to be a Policy Consultant, what skills do you need beyond a degree?

- By understanding the destination role, you gain clarity about the skills, education, experiences, and network you'll need.

VI
How to Select a Target Role That Fits You

Choosing a target role is not about picking a trendy job title. It's about discovering a role that resonates with your strengths, interests, and values, while also fitting into the real-world landscape of opportunities.

Here's how to break it down step by step:

1. Start With Self-Awareness

Before diving into job titles, get clear on who you are:

- What topics or activities energize you?
- Are you more creative, analytical, strategic, empathetic—or a mix?
- Do you enjoy working with people, systems, ideas, or things?
- What kinds of problems do you love solving?

Action Tip:
Make a list of moments when you felt most "in flow"—fully engaged in a task. These are clues to your core interests and potential functional fit (e.g., design, coding, storytelling, problem-solving, etc.).

2. Explore Role Categories

Once you have a sense of your personality and preferences, start exploring broad role types. For example:

- Tech roles (e.g., Software Engineer, Data Analyst, DevOps)
- Business roles (e.g., Consultant, Product Manager, Financial Analyst)
- Creative roles (e.g., Graphic Designer, Content Strategist, UX Designer)
- People-centric roles (e.g., HR Specialist, Community Manager, Sales Executive)
- Impact roles (e.g., Policy Researcher, Social Entrepreneur, Climate Analyst)

At this stage, it's not about choosing the perfect one—it's about noticing what sparks your curiosity.

Action Tip:
Look at LinkedIn profiles of professionals in fields you're curious about. See how their journeys unfolded and what roles they've held.

3. Validate with Exposure

You can't truly understand a role from a distance. The best way to gain clarity is through real-world exposure:

- Attend webinars or talks by people in those roles.
- Do mini-projects, online challenges, or simulations.
- Intern or volunteer in adjacent areas.

Conduct informational interviews with people working in your role of interest.

Action Tip:
Use platforms like Internshala, Forage, or LinkedIn Learning to do virtual experiences or shadowing projects that mimic real roles.

4. Align with Strengths and Skills

It's not enough to like a role—you also need to have (or develop) the right skills. Once you narrow down to a few potential roles, ask:

- What are the must-have hard skills (e.g., coding, data analysis, design tools)?
- What are the key soft skills (e.g., leadership, communication, time management)?
- Which of these do you already possess, and which do you need to build?

Action Tip:
Use tools like SkillUp by Simplilearn or Coursera Role Paths to see skill maps for popular roles.

5. Check for Market Demand

Your career should exist within the reality of today's job market. It's great to follow passion—but ensure the role also has growing demand, good entry-level access, and long-term potential.
Look for:

- Number of job openings
- Future growth projections
- Industries hiring for the role
- Transferability of the skills involved

Action Tip:
Visit sites like LinkedIn Jobs, Glassdoor, or Naukri.com, and type in your role to see job trends, salaries, and required skills.

6. Make a Shortlist and Test It

Now you should have 2–3 roles you're interested in. Create a mini-plan to explore each one more deeply over the next few months. Think of this as career prototyping—testing before committing.
Try:

- A project or challenge in each area
- Talking to 1–2 professionals in that role
- Taking 1 online course or certification
- Reflecting on which one excites you most after exposure

Outcome of This Step:

By the end of this process, you should have:

- A clear target role (or a strong first choice)
- A deeper understanding of the role's daily work
- A list of skills and experiences you need to pursue it
- Confidence in where to focus your energy next

VII
The Components of a Career Roadmap

Once you've identified a target role (or a few you're curious about), the next step is to build a roadmap that helps you reach it with confidence. A good career roadmap isn't just a plan—it's a system of progression. It breaks down the journey from beginner to professional into manageable parts.

Let's explore each component in detail:

1. Foundational Education

This is the academic or training ground where your journey begins. It could be a degree (like B.Tech, B.Sc, BBA), a diploma, or even online foundational courses. The key is to ensure your education is relevant to your role goals. For example, if you want to become a data scientist, a foundation in mathematics, statistics, or computer science is essential. For some roles (like content creator, UI/UX designer, or social worker), formal education can be flexible or non-traditional, provided you learn through other means (like bootcamps or community college).

Tip: Don't obsess over college rankings—focus on the skills and exposure the program gives you.

2. Core Skill Development

This includes both hard skills and soft skills needed for the target role. Hard skills: Technical abilities like coding, financial modeling, research writing, CAD, data visualization, etc. Soft skills: Communication, time management, teamwork, critical thinking, problem-solving. Build these skills through:

- Online platforms (Coursera, Udemy, Skillshare, etc.)
- Practical labs or makerspaces
- Peer learning groups and clubs
- Freelance projects or hackathons

Tip: Use project-based learning. For example, don't just "learn Python"—build something with it.

3. Hands-on Experience

Experience is the bridge between learning and employability.

- Internships (paid or unpaid)
- Freelance gigs
- Research assistant roles
- Volunteering
- Part-time projects
- Campus leadership roles

Real-world exposure helps you:

- Understand the actual day-to-day of the role
- Apply your learning in context
- Develop confidence and a network

Tip: Start early and don't wait for the "perfect internship." Even small projects help you build proof of work.

4. Portfolio or Proof of Work

For many modern roles, what you've done matters more than where you studied. A great portfolio showcases:

- Your projects (with problem, process, and outcome)
- Technical or creative skills in action
- Your unique approach or problem-solving style

Examples:

- Designers have visual portfolios.
- Writers/bloggers use personal websites.
- Developers use GitHub.
- Business students may have pitch decks or simulations.

Tip: Start a blog, Notion page, or LinkedIn series to document your growth. This becomes a magnet for future opportunities.

5. Certifications & Tools

Certifications are not always mandatory—but in tech, business, and analytics roles, they can give you an edge. Examples:

- Google Data Analytics Certificate
- AWS Cloud Practitioner
- HubSpot Inbound Marketing
- PMP (Project Management)
- Adobe Creative Suite

Also, learn tools common to your field:

- Figma, AutoCAD, Excel, Power BI, Tableau, Jira, etc.

Tip: Focus on one or two high-value tools, not every tool out there.

6. Networking & Mentorship

Opportunities often come through people, not portals. Networking helps you:

- Gain insights into roles/industries
- Find internships or projects
- Learn from others' journeys
- Stay motivated
- Build your network by:
- Reaching out on LinkedIn
- Attending virtual events, webinars, and hackathons
- Joining interest groups or communities (Discord, Reddit, Slack, WhatsApp)
- Asking thoughtful questions, not just favors

Tip: Always give before you ask—share your learnings, comment meaningfully, and offer to collaborate.

7. Entry-Level Role Awareness

Once you're prepared, you'll start seeking your first real job or startup role. It's essential to:

- Understand typical entry-level roles for your target position
- Know what recruiters look for in resumes and interviews
- Position your story (even if you're from a non-traditional background)

For example:

- Aspiring Product Managers often begin as Business Analysts, QA Engineers, or Operations Associates.
- Aspiring Researchers may begin as Research Interns or Technical Writers.

Tip: Track 10–15 job descriptions for your role and analyze skill/common themes. This will guide your resume and prep.

8. Continuous Learning Plan

Your roadmap doesn't end when you land your first job. Industries evolve, and so must you. Dedicate 1–2 hours a week to upskilling. Subscribe to top newsletters or YouTube channels in your field. Stay current with tech tools, trends, and industry news.

Tip: Build a "learning funnel"—Podcasts while commuting, reading 1 book a month, following thought leaders, etc.

Your Career GPS

A complete career roadmap includes:

- Education
- Skill-building
- Real-world experience
- Portfolio
- Certifications & tools
- Networking
- Entry-level job awareness
- Lifelong learning

This is not a one-size-fits-all path. You'll walk it at your own pace, based on your realities and resources. What matters is momentum and intentionality.

VIII
Tech Roles

1. *Software Developer / Engineer*

What They Do

- Build, test, and maintain software applications, websites, or system tools.

Foundational Education

- B.Tech / B.Sc in Computer Science, IT, or equivalent
- Diploma + coding bootcamps (valid alternative)

Skills to Build

- Languages: Python, Java, JavaScript, C++
- Tools: Git, GitHub, VS Code, APIs
- Frameworks: React, Node.js, Django, etc.
- Concepts: OOP, Data Structures, Algorithms

Portfolio Ideas

- Personal website or portfolio

- GitHub projects (e.g., task manager, e-commerce site, clone apps)
- Contributions to open-source

Certifications (Optional but Useful)

- Microsoft Azure Developer Associate
- AWS Developer Certification
- Google Associate Android Developer

Entry Roles

- Software Developer Intern
- Frontend/Backend Developer
- QA Tester
- Junior Engineer

2. Data Scientist / Analyst

What They Do

- Analyze data, generate insights, build predictive models, and guide decisions using data.

Foundational Education

- B.Tech in CS, Stats, Maths, or related fields
- Online certifications (Google Data Analytics, IBM Data Science)

Skills to Build

- Tools: Python, R, Excel, SQL
- Libraries: Pandas, NumPy, Matplotlib, Scikit-learn
- Concepts: Data Cleaning, Visualization, Statistics, ML Basics

Portfolio Ideas

- Kaggle competition participation
- Dashboards (Power BI, Tableau)
- Projects like predicting stock prices, sentiment analysis, etc.

Certifications

- Google Data Analytics
- IBM Data Science
- Tableau Specialist

Entry Roles

- Data Analyst Intern
- Junior Data Scientist
- Business Analyst

3. DevOps / Cloud Engineer

What They Do

- Automate deployment, monitor infrastructure, maintain server environments, ensure CI/CD processes.

Foundational Education

- B.Tech in IT/CS
- Linux/Networking knowledge is crucial

Skills to Build

- Linux, Bash scripting
- Git, Docker, Jenkins
- AWS/GCP/Azure services
- Kubernetes, Terraform

Certifications

- AWS Certified Solutions Architect
- Microsoft Azure Fundamentals
- Docker & Kubernetes Specializations

Portfolio Ideas

- Set up CI/CD pipelines
- Host websites using Docker containers
- Infrastructure as Code project

Entry Roles

- DevOps Intern
- Site Reliability Engineer (SRE) Associate
- Cloud Engineer Intern

4. Cybersecurity Specialist

What They Do

- Protect systems from threats, ensure compliance, monitor attacks, and build secure infrastructure.

Foundational Education

- B.Tech in Cybersecurity/IT
- Diploma + EC-Council/CompTIA courses

Skills to Build

- Networking, Firewalls
- Kali Linux, Wireshark, Burp Suite
- Ethical hacking basics
- SIEM tools

Certifications

- CEH (Certified Ethical Hacker)
- CompTIA Security+
- Cisco CCNA Security

Portfolio Ideas

- Simulated attack & penetration test reports
- Personal blog on threat detection
- Capture the Flag (CTF) achievements

Entry Roles

- Security Analyst Intern
- SOC Analyst
- Network Security Associate

5. UI/UX Designer

What They Do

- Design user-friendly interfaces, improve user journeys, and align aesthetics with usability.

Foundational Education

- Any bachelor's + design bootcamp
- B.Des or HCI-related course (optional)

Skills to Build

- Tools: Figma, Adobe XD, Sketch
- Concepts: Wireframes, User Personas, Prototyping
- HTML/CSS basics (optional but helpful)

Portfolio Ideas

- Case studies: redesigning apps/websites
- User journey mapping
- Mockups for products

Certifications

- Google UX Design Certificate
- Coursera / Interaction Design Foundation courses
- Entry Roles
- UX Intern
- Junior UI/UX Designer
- Product Designer Associate

6. Embedded Systems / IoT Engineer

What They Do

- Build software that interacts with hardware—especially for devices, smart systems, and robotics.

Foundational Education

- B.Tech in ECE, Mechatronics, or EE
- IoT/Embedded Systems specialization

Skills to Build

- C/C++, Embedded C
- Arduino, Raspberry Pi
- RTOS, Sensors, Actuators
- Circuit design and simulation

Portfolio Ideas

- IoT Smart Home system
- Temperature-controlled devices
- Raspberry Pi surveillance system

Certifications

- Embedded C training
- ARM Certification
- IoT Certification by NPTEL / Coursera

Entry Roles

- Embedded Systems Intern
- IoT Hardware Engineer
- R&D Assistant Engineer

7. Mechatronics / Robotics Engineer

What They Do

- Design intelligent machines combining mechanical, electrical, and software systems.

Foundational Education

- B.Tech in Mechatronics/Robotics
- Mechanical + Electronics + CS exposure

Skills to Build

- CAD (SolidWorks, AutoCAD)
- Arduino, PLCs
- Python/C++ for robotics
- ROS, OpenCV, MATLAB

Portfolio Ideas

- Line follower, robotic arm, automation systems
- 3D printed prototypes
- Simulations with Gazebo or Webots

Certifications

- Robotics Specialization – Coursera
- PLC Programming – Siemens / Allen Bradley

Entry Roles

- Robotics Intern
- Automation Engineer
- Mechatronics R&D Assistant

8. AI / Machine Learning Engineer

What They Do

- Build systems that learn from data—automated decision-making, predictions, and AI tools.

Foundational Education

- CS/IT B.Tech or Math-heavy background
- Online specializations from Stanford, MIT, or Google

Skills to Build

- Python, TensorFlow, PyTorch
- ML Algorithms, Deep Learning
- NLP, Computer Vision
- Model evaluation and deployment

Portfolio Ideas

- AI chatbot

- Image classifier or object detector
- NLP-based resume parser

Certifications

- DeepLearning.AI (Andrew Ng)
- TensorFlow Developer Certificate
- AWS Machine Learning Specialization

Entry Roles

- ML Engineer Intern
- Junior AI Developer
- NLP Intern

IX

Engineering Roles

1. Mechanical Engineer

What They Do

- Design, build, and maintain mechanical systems in industries ranging from automotive and aerospace to HVAC and energy.

Foundational Education

- B.E. / B.Tech in Mechanical Engineering
- M.E. / M.Tech for specialization (optional)

Skills to Build

- Solid mechanics, thermodynamics, machine design
- CAD tools: SolidWorks, CATIA, AutoCAD
- Simulation: ANSYS, MATLAB
- Hands-on manufacturing exposure (lathe, CNC, 3D printing)

Certifications

- NPTEL Mechanical Engineering
- Autodesk Certified Design Professional

Career Paths

- Maintenance Engineer → Design Engineer → Project Manager
- R&D Engineer → Technical Lead
- Entrepreneurship (product manufacturing / services)

2. Electrical/Electronics Engineer

What They Do

- Work on power systems, circuitry, embedded systems, automation, IoT, and control systems in everything from smart grids to medical devices.

Foundational Education

- B.E. / B.Tech in Electrical, Electronics or EEE
- M.Tech for VLSI, Embedded Systems, Power Systems, etc.

Skills to Build

- Circuit design, signal processing, control theory
- Embedded C, Arduino, Raspberry Pi
- Simulation tools: Proteus, Multisim, MATLAB/Simulink
- PLC, SCADA, and industrial automation tools

Certifications

- NI LabVIEW, Siemens PLC, Coursera IoT specializations

Career Paths

- Embedded Developer → Systems Engineer → Hardware Architect
- Power Engineer → Grid Manager
- Electronics Design Engineer → IoT Product Manager

3. Civil / Structural Engineer

What They Do

- Design and supervise infrastructure: buildings, roads, bridges, dams, and urban infrastructure.

Foundational Education

- B.E. / B.Tech in Civil Engineering
- M.Tech in Structural, Transportation, or Geotechnical Engineering

Skills to Build

- Surveying, RCC/steel structure design, geotechnics
- Software: STAAD Pro, AutoCAD Civil 3D, Revit, Primavera
- Project planning, estimation, construction management

Certifications

- CPWD Planning Certifications
- RERA or Smart City credentials

Career Paths

- Site Engineer → Structural Analyst → Construction Manager
- Government PWD roles → Infrastructure Consultant

4. Computer Science Engineer

What They Do

- Build software, applications, and computational systems. This field has expanded to include AI, cybersecurity, DevOps, cloud computing, and more.

Foundational Education

- B.E. / B.Tech in Computer Science / IT
- M.Tech or MSc in specializations (optional)

Skills to Build

- Programming: Python, Java, JavaScript, C++
- Data Structures & Algorithms
- Git, SQL, APIs, DevOps basics
- Web/App development, AI/ML, Blockchain, Cybersecurity

Certifications

- AWS/GCP Certifications, Meta Frontend, ML by Andrew Ng
- GitHub portfolio is vital

Career Paths

- Software Developer → Tech Lead → CTO
- ML Engineer → Data Scientist
- Full-Stack Developer → Product Architect

5. Mechatronics / Robotics Engineer

What They Do

- Design intelligent systems by combining mechanical, electronics, and software—automated machines, drones, and robotics.

Foundational Education

- B.E. / B.Tech in Mechatronics / Robotics / Automation
- M.Tech in Robotics / AI / Industrial Automation

Skills to Build

- Arduino, Raspberry Pi, sensors, actuators
- Control systems, embedded systems, Python/C++

- Robot Operating System (ROS), CAD for robotics
- Machine vision, path planning algorithms

Certifications

- Udacity Robotics Nanodegree
- ROS and OpenCV courses

Career Paths

- Robotics Engineer → Automation Lead
- Drone Developer → AI Robotics Researcher

6. Chemical / Process Engineer

What They Do

- Work in petrochemicals, pharmaceuticals, manufacturing, and food processing—designing and optimizing chemical processes.

Foundational Education

- B.Tech in Chemical Engineering
- M.Tech in Process Design / Petrochemicals / Biotech

Skills to Build

- Mass & heat transfer, reactor design, process control
- Aspen Plus, HYSYS, ChemCAD software
- Safety protocols and quality standards (ISO, GMP)

Certifications

- Six Sigma, OSHA Safety
- AIChE (American Institute of Chemical Engineers)

Career Paths

- Process Engineer → Plant Manager
- Quality Control Analyst → Compliance Lead

7. Renewable Energy / Environmental Engineer

What They Do

- Design systems for solar, wind, biofuels, waste-to-energy, and sustainability-focused infrastructure.

  Foundational Education

- B.Tech in Energy, Environmental, or Mechanical
- Specialization in Renewable Energy / Sustainability

  Skills to Build

- PV system design, energy audit
- Environmental impact analysis
- SCADA, RETScreen, PVsyst tools
- Regulations: ISO 14001, ECBC, GRIHA

  Certifications

- NISE Solar Certification
- LEED Green Associate

  Career Paths

- Solar Design Engineer → Renewable Energy Consultant
- Environmental Auditor → ESG Manager

8. Design / Product Development Engineer

What They Do

- Turn ideas into manufacturable products. Work on prototyping, design thinking, testing, and product-market fit.

Foundational Education

- B.E. in Mechanical, Mechatronics, or Product Design
- M.Des (Design) or M.Tech in Product Engineering

Skills to Build

- CAD (SolidWorks, Fusion360), prototyping (3D printing, CNC)
- Design thinking, human-centered design
- Materials knowledge and DFMA
- Team collaboration with marketing/R&D

Certifications

- IDF Design Thinking Certificate
- Autodesk Design Professional

Career Paths

- Product Designer → Lead R&D Engineer
- Innovation Specialist → Industrial Design Consultant

X
Healthcare & Life Sciences Roles

1. Doctor / Physician (Clinical Practice)

- Role Focus: Diagnosing, treating, and managing patients through direct medical care.

  Education Path (India Example):

- Complete 12th with PCB (Physics, Chemistry, Biology).
- Clear NEET exam → MBBS (5.5 years).
- Postgraduate specialization (MD/MS/DNB) in desired field (e.g., Pediatrics, Surgery).
- Super-specialization (DM/MCh) for advanced roles.

  Career Options:

- Hospital Practice, Private Clinic, Government Healthcare, Telemedicine, or Research.

  Growth:

- Senior Consultant → Head of Department → Hospital Director or Research Clinician.

2. Nurse / Allied Health Professional

- Role Focus: Providing support in medical settings—patient care, diagnostics, therapy, and rehabilitation.

Education Path:

- Nursing: B.Sc. Nursing / GNM → M.Sc. Nursing (optional).
- Allied Health: UG in Physiotherapy, Radiology, Anesthesia, Occupational Therapy, etc.
- Diplomas or certifications in specialized fields (e.g., Critical Care, Dialysis, NICU).

Opportunities:

- Hospitals, Diagnostic Centers, Sports Teams, Elderly Care Homes, Telehealth.

Growth:

- Senior Clinical Roles, Teaching, Healthcare Admin, or Clinical Research.

3. Medical Researcher / Life Sciences Scientist

- Role Focus: Conducting scientific research in biology, genetics, pathology, or drug discovery.

Education Path:

- UG: B.Sc. in Biotechnology, Microbiology, Zoology, Biochemistry.
- PG: M.Sc. / M.Tech in Life Sciences / Biotechnology.

- Ph.D. in a specialized area (e.g., Cancer Biology, Molecular Genetics).

Research Experience:

- Work in labs, publish in journals, present at conferences.
- Apply for research grants or join CSIR, DBT, ICMR projects.

Careers:

- R&D in pharma/biotech firms, government labs, academic institutions.

Growth:

- Lead Researcher → Principal Investigator → Scientific Director.

4. *Pharmacist / Pharmaceutical Scientist*

- Role Focus: Medication dispensing, safety, and pharmaceutical innovation.

Pharmacist Path:

- D.Pharm / B.Pharm → M.Pharm (optional) → Register with Pharmacy Council.
- Work in hospitals, retail pharmacies, or pharmaceutical sales.

Pharma R&D Path:

- B.Pharm / B.Sc. Chemistry → M.Pharm / M.Sc. → Pharma research roles.
- Focus on drug formulation, toxicology, regulatory affairs, or quality control.

Growth:

- Senior Scientist, Production Head, Clinical Pharmacologist, Regulatory Lead.

5. Public Health Professional

- Role Focus: Managing population health, disease prevention, policy, and health systems.

Academic Path:

- UG in Medicine, Life Sciences, or Sociology.
- Master's in Public Health (MPH), Epidemiology, Health Policy, or Global Health.

Work Sectors:

- NGOs, government programs (NHM, WHO), international orgs (UNICEF, Gates Foundation).

Roles:

- Epidemiologist, Health Program Manager, Policy Analyst, Health Educator.

Growth:

- Become Regional Program Lead, Health Economist, or Health Systems Advisor.

6. Mental Health Professional

- Role Focus: Supporting mental wellness through counseling, therapy, or psychiatric care.

Paths:

- Clinical Psychologist: UG + PG in Psychology → M.Phil in Clinical Psychology.
- Psychiatrist: MBBS → MD Psychiatry.
- Counsellor: Diploma or PG Diploma in Counseling Psychology, Social Work, or Rehabilitation.

Opportunities:

- Work in schools, hospitals, private practice, or mental health NGOs.

Growth:

- Start own clinic, conduct training, or specialize in adolescent, trauma, or addiction counseling.

7. Medical Technologist / Lab Technician

- Role Focus: Running diagnostics, imaging, pathology, and lab management.

Education Path:

- Diploma or B.Sc. in Medical Laboratory Technology, Radiology, Imaging, etc.
- Specialized certifications in MRI, CT, Blood Bank, etc.

Career Path:

- Diagnostic Labs (Thyrocare, SRL), Hospitals, Research Centers.

Growth:

- Lab In-Charge, Quality Manager, or Diagnostic Lab Entrepreneur.

8. Healthcare Administration / Hospital Management

- Role Focus: Overseeing hospital operations, compliance, resource planning, and patient experience.

Education Path:

- UG in any stream → MBA in Healthcare Management / Hospital Administration.
- Courses from institutes like IHMR, TISS, IIMs (Healthcare electives).

Career Opportunities:

- Hospitals, Health Insurance firms, Government Health Missions.

Growth:

- Manager → Operations Head → Hospital CEO or Healthcare Consultant.

9. Medical Writer / Health Communicator

- Role Focus: Writing scientific/medical content for education, awareness, or compliance.

Education Path:

- Background in Life Sciences, Pharma, or Journalism.
- Certification in medical writing (e.g., AMWA, MedComms).

Work Areas:

- Research papers, patient education content, pharma communications, regulatory documents.

Opportunities:

- Freelance, work with publishing firms, health-tech startups, pharma companies.

XI
Commerce Roles

1. Chartered Accountant (CA)

- Role Focus: Managing audits, tax planning, financial compliance, accounting, and advisory for businesses.

  Education Path (India):

- After 12th: Register with ICAI → Clear CA Foundation → CA Intermediate → Articleship (3 years) → CA Final.
- After graduation (Commerce): Direct entry to Intermediate level.

  Career Opportunities:

- Audit firms (Big 4), corporates, startups, public sector units, independent practice.

  Growth Path:

- CA → Finance Controller → CFO or start your own consultancy.

2. Company Secretary (CS)

- Role Focus: Legal compliance, corporate governance, company law advisory, and liaison with regulatory bodies.

Pathway (India):

- Foundation → Executive → Professional Programme → Training.
- Conducted by the ICSI (Institute of Company Secretaries of India).

Work Domains:

- Listed companies, MNCs, secretarial firms, or start as an independent CS.

Growth:

- Company Secretary → Legal/Compliance Head → Director – Legal Affairs.

3. Cost & Management Accountant (CMA)

- Role Focus: Costing, budgeting, internal audits, and strategic financial management.

Education Path:

- Register with ICMAI → Foundation → Intermediate → Final → Practical Training.

Industry Demand:

- Manufacturing, consulting, FMCG, telecom, or any industry with large financial operations.

Growth Path:

- Cost Analyst → Cost Controller → CFO.

4. Economist / Policy Analyst

- Role Focus: Analyzing data to study economic trends, and advise policy, business strategy, or development.

Academic Route:

- UG in Economics → PG in Economics / Public Policy / Development Studies.
- Consider institutes like DSE, ISI, Ashoka, IGIDR, or international (LSE, Harvard Kennedy School).

Careers:

- Think tanks, NITI Aayog, RBI, international organizations (UN, IMF, World Bank), consultancies.

Growth:

- Analyst → Economist → Policy Advisor / Economic Consultant.

5. Financial Analyst / Investment Banker / Equity Research

- Role Focus: Analysing markets, financial statements, valuing companies, and making investment recommendations.

Academic Path:

- UG in Commerce / BBA / Economics → MBA (Finance) or CFA.
- CFA (Chartered Financial Analyst): Globally recognized credential (3 levels).

Domains:

- Investment banks, hedge funds, mutual funds, fintech, venture capital.

Growth:

- Analyst → Associate → VP → Director → Managing Director.

6. Banking & Insurance Professional

- Role Focus: Retail/corporate banking, risk assessment, customer relationship, and loan/insurance product management.

Banking Path:

- UG degree → Clear bank exams (SBI PO, IBPS) or private sector recruitment.
- Consider PGDBF or MBA in Banking/Finance for managerial roles.

Insurance Sector:

- Join as agent, underwriter, claims manager, actuary, or business development executive.

Growth:

- Assistant Manager → Branch Manager → Zonal Head → General Manager.

7. E-commerce / Digital Business Manager

- Role Focus: Managing online businesses, digital marketing, customer experience, and logistics.

Learning Path:

- UG + Certifications in E-commerce, SEO/SEM, UI/UX, Product Management.
- Digital Marketing: Google Digital Garage, HubSpot Academy, Meta Blueprint.

Careers:

- Work with Flipkart, Amazon, D2C brands, or build your own store on Shopify.

Growth:

- Marketing Exec → E-commerce Manager → Digital Business Head.

8. Tax Consultant / GST Practitioner

- Role Focus: Tax planning, GST filing, corporate taxation, and advisory.

Learning Path:

- UG + Taxation specialization (via CA, CMA, LLB or independent).
- Become a certified GST Practitioner (via GSTN portal in India).

Work Domains:

- Start own consultancy, work with CA firms, tax-tech startups.

9. Lawyer – Corporate / Tax / Business Law

- Role Focus: Representing businesses legally in matters of contracts, mergers, tax disputes, compliance.

Education Path:

- 5-year integrated LLB (after 12th Commerce) or 3-year LLB (after graduation).
- Specialize in Corporate Law, Tax Law, or IPR.
- Consider top law colleges: NLUs, Symbiosis, Jindal.

Growth:

- Associate → Senior Associate → Partner or In-house Counsel / Legal Head.

10. Entrepreneur / Startup Founder

- Role Focus: Creating and running a business – from idea to revenue and scaling.

Preparation:

- UG in any field + learning through incubation programs (e.g., IIMs, NSRCEL, Y Combinator).
- Build skills in digital marketing, product design, finance, team management.

Support:

- Leverage Startup India, fundraisers, startup mentors, networking events.

Growth:

- Solo founder → Team builder → Scaled startup → Acquisition / IPO.

11. Business & Data Analytics Professional

- Role Focus: Using data to drive decision-making in finance, HR, marketing, or operations.

Skills Needed:

- Excel, SQL, Power BI/Tableau, Python (optional), critical thinking.
- UG → Analytics Certification (Google Data Analytics, IBM, Great Learning).

Career Options:

- Analyst → Data-driven roles in finance, retail, HR, marketing, operations.

XII
Management & Leadership Roles

1. Business / Strategy Consultant

What They Do

- They analyze business problems, collect and interpret data, and suggest strategic solutions to improve profitability and efficiency.

Foundational Education

- Bachelor's in Business, Economics, Engineering, or related
- MBA (for consulting, strategy) is often preferred

Skills to Build

- Excel, SQL, Tableau, Power BI
- Business analytics, problem-solving frameworks (SWOT, BCG Matrix, Porter's Five Forces)
- Presentation skills, stakeholder management

Certifications

- Google Data Analytics
- Certified Business Analysis Professional (CBAP)

Career Path

- Junior Analyst → Consultant → Engagement Manager → Partner
- Strategy Intern → Analyst → Business Strategist

2. *Product Manager (PM)*

What They Do

- PMs manage the lifecycle of a product from idea to launch. They sit at the intersection of business, technology, and users.

Foundational Education

- Any bachelor's degree; technical background helps
- MBA or Product Management bootcamps (optional but useful)

Skills to Build

- User research, market research, agile frameworks
- Roadmapping, UI/UX basics, wireframing (Figma, Miro)
- Communication with cross-functional teams (engineering, marketing)

Certifications

- Product School
- Pragmatic Institute
- Reforge PM

Career Path

- Associate PM → Product Manager → Senior PM → Director / CPO

3. Operations Manager

What They Do

- Plan, optimize, and manage daily operations in manufacturing, logistics, services, and supply chains to improve efficiency and reduce cost.

Foundational Education

- Bachelor's in Engineering, Operations, or Business
- MBA in Operations / SCM (preferred for higher roles)

Skills to Build

- Process optimization, lean manufacturing, Six Sigma
- ERP systems, project planning (Primavera, MS Project)
- Vendor management, budgeting, quality control

Certifications

- Six Sigma (Green/Black Belt)
- PMP or CPIM (APICS)

Career Path

- Operations Trainee → Ops Executive → Plant Manager → COO

4. Sales & Marketing Professional

What They Do

- Sales and marketing professionals generate demand, drive revenue, build brand identity, and align products to customer needs.

Foundational Education

- Bachelor's in Business, Commerce, or Communications

- MBA in Marketing / Digital Marketing specialization

Skills to Build

- Sales funnels, CRM tools (Salesforce, Zoho)
- SEO, SEM, Google Ads, social media marketing
- Email marketing, copywriting, campaign analysis

Certifications

- Google Digital Marketing
- HubSpot Academy
- Meta Blueprint

Career Path

- Sales Executive → Marketing Manager → Brand Head
- BDE → Area Sales Manager → VP Sales

5. Human Resources (HR) / People Manager

What They Do

- Manage hiring, training, performance, retention, and workplace culture to build high-performing, happy teams.

Foundational Education

- BBA / BCom with HR electives
- MBA in HR or Organizational Psychology

Skills to Build

- Talent acquisition, L&D, HR analytics
- Conflict resolution, emotional intelligence
- HRMS tools: SAP, Workday, Zoho People

Certifications

- SHRM-CP or PHR
- LinkedIn Learning HR courses

Career Path

- HR Executive → HRBP → HR Manager → CHRO

6. Entrepreneur / Startup Founder

What They Do

- Founders identify real-world problems, build solutions, and create organizations to deliver them at scale—often in tech or impact spaces.

Foundational Education

- Any degree, but a mix of tech + business helps
- Programs like IIM's IEV, Stanford Seed Spark, Y Combinator

Skills to Build

- Problem solving, MVP building, pitching, team hiring
- Basic finance, product-market fit, growth hacking
- Fundraising, storytelling, legal compliance

Certifications / Resources

- Startup India Learning Program
- Y Combinator Startup School
- Stanford eCorner

Career Path

- Ideation → Prototyping → Fundraising → Scaling → Exit / IPO

7. *Finance & Investment Professional*

What They Do

- Handle money movement—investments, risk management, budgeting, capital allocation, and wealth creation.

Foundational Education

- B.Com / BBA in Finance
- MBA Finance or Chartered Financial Analyst (CFA)

Skills to Build

- Financial modeling, valuation, Excel, PowerPoint
- Knowledge of equity, debt, mutual funds, crypto
- Understanding taxation, accounting, risk

Certifications

- CFA, FRM, NSE Certification in Financial Markets
- Wall Street Prep / CFI Finance Modeling

Career Path

- Analyst → Investment Banker → Portfolio Manager
- Finance Executive → CFO

8. *Supply Chain / Logistics Manager*

What They Do

- Ensure timely sourcing, movement, and delivery of products with minimal cost and optimal efficiency.

Foundational Education

- Bachelor's in Logistics, Operations, or Engineering
- MBA or PGD in SCM

Skills to Build

- Demand forecasting, inventory control
- SAP SCM, Oracle NetSuite, WMS tools
- Vendor & contract negotiation

Certifications

- CSCP (Certified Supply Chain Professional)
- APICS Logistics certifications

Career Path

- Logistics Coordinator → SCM Manager → VP Logistics

XIII

Education, Academia & Research Roles

1. School Educator

- Role Focus: Teaching children and adolescents in schools, focusing on foundational learning, values, and holistic development.

Education Path:

- Complete a Bachelor's Degree in Education (B.Ed) or subject-specific UG + B.Ed.
- Optionally, pursue a Master's in Education (M.Ed) or subject area (MA, MSc).

Certifications:

- Pass state/national-level teaching eligibility tests (CTET, TET).
- Special education or early childhood certifications (if relevant).

Build Experience:

- Start as an assistant teacher or trainee.

- Engage in workshops, classroom innovations, and parent-community involvement.

Growth Path:

- Become head of department, principal, or curriculum planner.
- Pursue education leadership programs or international teaching fellowships.

2. College/University Faculty

- Role Focus: Teaching undergraduate or postgraduate students, academic mentoring, and subject research.

Education Path:

- Complete UG and PG in chosen subject.
- Qualify NET/SET (for India) or equivalent eligibility for lectureship.
- Pursue a Ph.D. for academic advancement.

Build Research Skills:

- Publish research papers, attend academic conferences.
- Collaborate with other institutions or international faculty.

Career Progression:

- Start as Assistant Professor → Associate Professor → Professor.
- Take on administrative roles like Dean, HOD, or Academic Council Member.

3. Educational Researcher

- Role Focus: Studying learning systems, pedagogical methods, educational psychology, and systemic outcomes.

Academic Path:

- UG/PG in Education, Psychology, Sociology, or subject specialization.
- M.Phil or Ph.D. in Education or Learning Sciences.

Research Experience:

- Work under a senior researcher, publish in journals, apply for grants.
- Learn statistical methods (SPSS, R) and research tools.

Career Tracks:

- Work with NGOs, policy think tanks, international organizations (UNESCO, UNICEF).
- Become Research Fellow, Education Policy Analyst, or Lead Evaluator.

4. *Curriculum Designer / Instructional Designer*

- Role Focus: Designing modern, outcome-based, inclusive, and innovative learning content.

Education Path:

- UG/PG in Education, Learning Design, Psychology, or Liberal Arts.
- Take certification courses in Instructional Design (e.g., IDOL, ATD).

Skill Development:

- Learn tools like Articulate, Canva, Genially, Storyline, LMS tools (Moodle, Blackboard).
- Build experience through freelance curriculum projects or internships.

Career Progression:

- Work with schools, EdTech companies, publishing houses.
- Progress to Lead Instructional Designer, Product Manager – Learning Content, or Consultant.

5. EdTech Professional

- Role Focus: Using technology to revolutionize education delivery, accessibility, and personalization.

Diverse Entry Points:

- Can come from tech (CS, IT), education, design, or product backgrounds.
- Upskill with EdTech-specific courses (AI in Education, Learning Analytics).

Popular Roles:

- Product Manager, Learning Experience Designer, Academic Strategist, EdTech Founder.

Platforms to Work With:

- Khan Academy, Unacademy, Coursera, or start your own EdTech initiative.

Growth:

- Combine user feedback, pedagogy, and data insights to innovate.
- Build cross-functional skills (tech + learning + business).

6. Policy Advisor / Education Consultant

- Role Focus: Working with governments, NGOs, or international bodies to reform education systems.

Education Background:

- Strong grounding in education, sociology, public policy, or development studies.
- Master's in Public Policy, Education Policy, or related areas (e.g., TISS, Azim Premji, LSE, Harvard GSE).

Experience:

- Work in research-based roles or field interventions.
- Build familiarity with policy papers, data collection, community models.

Growth Opportunities:

- Roles at UNESCO, Brookings, NITI Aayog, state education missions.
- Can also work independently as a consultant for policy evaluation or reform.

7. Independent Scholar / Public Educator

- Role Focus: Educating and influencing through public speaking, content creation, online education, or books.

Flexible Entry:

- Anyone with deep knowledge in a domain + ability to communicate and educate.
- Strong content skills (writing, speaking, video creation).

Platform Building:

- Grow a blog, YouTube channel, podcast, or write for platforms like Medium or LinkedIn.
- Develop courses on Teachable, Gumroad, or host webinars.

Revenue Streams:

- Paid talks, books, consulting, Patreon, cohort-based courses.

Examples:

- Dr. Jordan Peterson (Psychology/Public Education), Sal Khan (Khan Academy), or Deepak Ramola (Project Fuel).

XIV

Government, Policy & Civil Service Roles

1. Civil Services (IAS, IPS, IRS, IFS, etc.)

What They Do

- Form the administrative backbone of the country. IAS officers manage districts, policies, and ministries; IPS officers lead police and law enforcement; IRS handles tax administration; IFS represents India internationally.

Foundational Education

- Bachelor's degree in any field
- UPSC Civil Services Exam is mandatory (Prelims → Mains → Interview)

Skills to Build

- General Studies (History, Polity, Economics, Science)
- Current affairs, ethical reasoning
- Analytical writing & critical thinking

- Decision-making, leadership

Prep Resources

- NCERTs, Yojana, PIB, The Hindu
- Coaching (online or offline), mock tests
- Ethics and essay practice

Entry Roles

- Indian Administrative Service (IAS) Officer
- Indian Police Service (IPS) Officer
- Indian Foreign Service (IFS) Officer

2. Public Policy Analyst

What They Do

- Design, evaluate, and improve policies for governments, NGOs, think tanks, or international bodies like UNDP. Involves data analysis, public consultations, and legislation review.

Foundational Education

- Degree in Economics, Political Science, Law, or Public Policy
- Master's in Public Policy (MPP) is preferred but not essential

Skills to Build

- Policy research & drafting
- Impact assessment and governance models
- Quantitative skills (Excel, STATA, R)
- Communication with stakeholders

Portfolio Ideas

- Policy briefs, white papers

- Legislative recommendations
- Volunteer policy internships

Certifications

- Harvard / LSE Public Policy courses
- J-PAL, ISPP India Fellowships

Entry Roles

- Policy Research Associate
- Legislative Assistant (LAMP Fellow)
- Development Analyst

3. Indian Engineering Services (IES)

What They Do

- Technical management for large-scale government projects in Railways, Roadways, Telecom, Power, etc. Bridge engineers with policy makers.

Foundational Education

- B.Tech in Civil, Mechanical, Electrical, or Electronics
- Must clear UPSC Engineering Services Examination (ESE)

Skills to Build

- Core technical concepts
- Engineering aptitude and ethics
- Decision-making in public infrastructure
- Communication and leadership

Entry Roles

- Assistant Executive Engineer
- Indian Railway Service of Engineers

- Central Engineering Services

4. *Judicial Services / Legal Officer*

What They Do

- Interpret and enforce laws. Judicial officers include magistrates, judges, and legal researchers; legal officers serve in government ministries or PSUs.

Foundational Education

- LLB (3 or 5-year)
- Clear Judicial Services Exam (for judge/magistrate)

Skills to Build

- Constitutional, criminal, and civil law
- Case analysis and legal writing
- Courtroom procedure and ethics
- Public speaking and interpretation

Prep Resources

- Bare Acts, case laws
- Mock court practice
- Legal internships or moot courts

Entry Roles

- Civil Judge / Judicial Magistrate
- Legal Officer in PSU
- Government Advocate

5. Government Researcher / Scientist (ISRO, DRDO, CSIR, etc.)

What They Do

- Conduct scientific R&D in defense, space, biotechnology, energy, and public health. These roles are highly respected and contribute to strategic development.

Foundational Education

- B.Sc / M.Sc or B.Tech / M.Tech in relevant fields
- GATE exam often required

Skills to Build

- Research methodology and lab techniques
- Programming, simulations, modeling
- Report writing and publications
- Team collaboration and experimentation

Certifications

- NET/JRF, GATE for eligibility
- Specializations via NPTEL, AICTE

Entry Roles

- Junior Research Fellow (JRF)
- Scientist B (ISRO, DRDO, BARC)
- Technical Officer in CSIR

6. Urban Planner / Development Officer

What They Do

- Design and regulate urban infrastructure: housing, transport, water systems, and sustainability. Work with municipal bodies or national planning agencies.

Foundational Education

- Architecture, Civil Engineering, or Urban Planning
- Master's in Urban / Rural / Regional Planning (optional)

Skills to Build

- AutoCAD, GIS, Smart City concepts
- Urban sociology, development economics
- Environmental law, land policies
- Public consultation and reporting

Certifications

- IGNOU or CEPT planning courses
- World Bank Smart City Toolkit

Entry Roles

- Assistant Town Planner
- Project Associate (Smart Cities Mission)
- Housing Development Officer

7. Diplomats / Foreign Affairs Officers

What They Do

- Represent India abroad, manage bilateral/multilateral relationships, and protect Indian interests in international forums.

Foundational Education

- Any Bachelor's degree

- Entry through UPSC Civil Services → IFS

Skills to Build

- International Relations, Foreign Policy
- Cultural sensitivity, languages
- Protocol, negotiation, writing dispatches
- Crisis handling, analysis

Training Ground

- Foreign Service Institute (post-selection)
- Study of global diplomacy and trade relations

Entry Roles

- Third Secretary
- Assistant High Commission Attaché

XV
Creative & Content Roles

1. Content Writer / Copywriter

What They Do

- Craft written content for websites, blogs, ads, and social media to inform, engage, or persuade audiences. Copywriters focus on persuasive writing, while content writers focus on value-driven storytelling.

Foundational Education

- Bachelor's in English, Journalism, Communications, or any field with a strong writing interest
- No formal degree mandatory

Skills to Build

- Grammar, clarity, persuasive writing
- SEO content strategy
- Tools: Grammarly, Surfer SEO, Hemingway, ChatGPT
- Research & storytelling

Portfolio Ideas

- Medium or personal blog
- Mock website copy and ad campaigns
- Guest posts or freelance gigs

Certifications

- HubSpot Content Marketing
- Copywriting Courses (Udemy, Coursera)
- SEMrush Content Toolkit

Entry Roles

- Content Writer Intern
- Junior Copywriter
- Blog Contributor

2. Graphic Designer / Visual Artist

What They Do

- Use visual tools to communicate ideas—logos, ads, infographics, illustrations, packaging, branding.

Foundational Education

- Bachelor's in Design, Fine Arts, Visual Communication
- Or self-taught with a strong portfolio

Skills to Build

- Adobe Suite (Photoshop, Illustrator, InDesign)
- Canva, Figma
- Color theory, typography, branding
- Visual storytelling and layout

Portfolio Ideas

- Logo redesigns
- Personal branding projects
- Posters, banners, brochures

Certifications

- Coursera Visual Design
- Adobe Creative Certifications
- Domestika/Skillshare Design Series

Entry Roles

- Junior Graphic Designer
- Creative Intern
- Visual Content Assistant

3. UI/UX Designer

What They Do

- Design user-friendly and visually appealing digital interfaces. Focus on user behavior, wireframes, design systems, and usability testing.

Foundational Education

- Bachelor's in Design, HCI, Psychology, or Tech
- Self-taught pathways widely accepted with strong portfolio

Skills to Build

- Wireframing tools: Figma, Adobe XD, Sketch
- User research, personas, journey mapping
- Design systems and accessibility
- Prototyping and usability testing

Portfolio Ideas

- Case studies with problem statements
- App/web redesign projects
- UX research findings and solutions

Certifications

- Google UX Design Certificate
- Interaction Design Foundation
- CareerFoundry / Coursera UX Programs

Entry Roles

- UI/UX Designer Intern
- Junior Designer
- User Research Assistant

4. Filmmaker / Video Editor / Animator

What They Do

- Create compelling videos, documentaries, advertisements, and animations. Involves storytelling, visuals, editing, and often sound design.

Foundational Education

- Film Studies, Media, Animation, or related degrees
- Many successful creators are self-taught

Skills to Build

- Adobe Premiere Pro, Final Cut Pro, After Effects
- Storyboarding, cinematography basics
- Animation (2D/3D), VFX
- Scripting, pacing, transitions

Portfolio Ideas

- Short films / YouTube channel
- Animated explainer videos
- Freelance or client projects

Certifications

- Video Editing & Motion Graphics (Skillshare, Domestika)
- Film Direction or Animation Courses
- YouTube Creator Academy

Entry Roles

- Video Editor
- Assistant Director / Scriptwriter
- Motion Graphics Intern

5. Social Media Manager / Influencer

What They Do

- Manage and grow a brand's online presence. Includes planning, posting, engaging, analytics, and sometimes personal branding as a creator.

Foundational Education

- No formal degree required
- Background in Communication, Marketing, or Design helps

Skills to Build

- Platform-specific content (Instagram, LinkedIn, YouTube)
- Tools: Buffer, Canva, Hootsuite, Later
- Copywriting, storytelling, community management
- Understanding of trends, virality, and engagement metrics

Portfolio Ideas

- Manage social media for a startup or NGO
- Personal brand or page growth
- Campaign reports with analytics

Certifications

- Meta Blueprint
- Hootsuite Social Marketing
- HubSpot Social Media Strategy

Entry Roles

- Social Media Intern
- Community Manager
- Content Strategist

6. Photographer

What They Do

- Capture visual moments—commercial, fashion, wedding, product, or art photography.

Foundational Education

- Courses in photography, design, or self-taught
- Art and storytelling instincts are key

Skills to Build

- DSLR/mirrorless camera handling
- Composition, lighting, editing (Lightroom, Photoshop)
- Niche understanding: Portraits, Landscape, Product
- Business and client communication

Portfolio Ideas

- Thematic photo collections
- Event shoots or creative series
- Instagram as a portfolio

Certifications

- Udemy Photography Masterclass
- National Geographic or Canon Photography Courses
- Workshops and field projects

Entry Roles

- Photography Assistant
- Freelance gigs
- Studio intern

7. Creative Director

What They Do

- Lead the overall creative vision of a brand, film, campaign, or product. Think strategy, storytelling, visuals, and brand tone.

Foundational Education

- Degrees in Communication, Design, Advertising, or Media
- Strong experience in design, content, or film creation

Skills to Build

- Creative thinking, leadership, branding
- Understanding of multiple creative disciplines
- Project management and campaign planning
- Client pitching and concept selling

Portfolio Ideas

- End-to-end campaigns
- Brand guides and identity projects
- Art direction samples

Certifications

- Branding & Art Direction (Domestika, Coursera)
- Strategic Creative Thinking (LinkedIn Learning)

Entry Roles

- Art Director
- Campaign Manager
- Lead Designer / Writer

XVI
Impact-Driven Roles

1. Social Entrepreneur / Impact Innovator

What They Do

- Founders who create ventures aimed at solving social problems—such as poverty, education, healthcare—with innovative business models.

Foundational Education

- Business, Social Sciences, or STEM with social impact focus
- Specialized programs: Ashoka U, Schwab Foundation courses

Skills to Build

- Design thinking, human-centered innovation
- Fundraising (grants, impact investors), stakeholder engagement
- Measuring impact (Social Return on Investment - SROI)

Certifications / Resources

- Stanford Social Innovation Review courses
- Echoing Green Fellowship

Career Path

- Idea incubation → Pilot program → Scaling impact → Global partnerships

2. Sustainability Manager / Environmental Consultant

What They Do

- They help organizations reduce environmental footprint through sustainable practices and compliance with regulations.

Foundational Education

- Environmental Science, Engineering, or Business with Sustainability focus

Skills to Build

- Carbon accounting, lifecycle analysis
- Sustainability reporting (GRI, SASB standards)
- Policy compliance, stakeholder management

Certifications

- LEED Accredited Professional
- GRI Certified Sustainability Professional

Career Path

- Sustainability Analyst → Consultant → Manager → Director of Sustainability

3. Policy Analyst / Public Affairs Specialist

What They Do

- Research, develop, and advocate for policies that address social, economic, or environmental issues.

Foundational Education

- Political Science, Economics, Public Administration

Skills to Build

- Research, data analysis, legislative knowledge
- Writing policy briefs, stakeholder engagement
- Public speaking, lobbying

Certifications

- Certified Public Policy Analyst (CPPA)
- Courses in governance & diplomacy

Career Path

- Research Assistant → Analyst → Policy Advisor → Director / Lobbyist

4. Nonprofit Manager / NGO Leader

What They Do

- Manage nonprofit organizations focusing on education, health, poverty alleviation, or human rights.

Foundational Education

- Social Work, Development Studies, or Business Admin with nonprofit focus

Skills to Build

- Fundraising, grant writing, program management
- Volunteer coordination, monitoring & evaluation
- Financial management, compliance

Certifications

- Certified Nonprofit Professional (CNP)
- Fundraising Management Certification

Career Path

- Program Coordinator → Manager → Executive Director / CEO

5. *Corporate Social Responsibility (CSR) Manager*

What They Do

- Develop and implement CSR initiatives that align business goals with social and environmental responsibility.

Foundational Education

- Business, Communications, or Sustainability

Skills to Build

- Stakeholder analysis, impact measurement
- Reporting frameworks, communications strategy
- Partnerships with NGOs and governments

Certifications

- CSR-P (CSR Practitioner) Certification
- ISO 26000 Training

Career Path

- CSR Executive → Manager → Director of CSR

6. Data Scientist / Analyst for Social Good

What They Do

- Use data to solve societal problems like public health, education, and disaster response.

Foundational Education

- Statistics, Computer Science, Data Science

Skills to Build

- Python/R, machine learning, data visualization
- Ethical AI, privacy compliance
- Domain knowledge in social sectors

Certifications

- IBM Data Science Professional Certificate
- DataCamp Social Impact courses

Career Path

- Junior Analyst → Data Scientist → Lead Analyst → Chief Data Officer

7. Urban Planner / Smart City Specialist

What They Do

- Design sustainable, efficient urban environments leveraging technology and policy.

Foundational Education

- Urban Planning, Civil Engineering, Architecture

Skills to Build

- GIS software, data analytics
- Urban design principles, transportation systems
- Public engagement and policy development

Certifications

- American Institute of Certified Planners (AICP)
- Smart Cities certification programs

Career Path

- Assistant Planner → Urban Planner → Project Manager → Chief Urban Strategist

8. Renewable Energy Specialist

What They Do

- Focus on development, implementation, and management of renewable energy projects—solar, wind, bioenergy.

Foundational Education

- Electrical / Mechanical Engineering, Environmental Science

Skills to Build

- Energy modeling, grid integration
- Regulatory frameworks, project finance
- Technical design and maintenance

Certifications

- NABCEP Solar PV Certification
- Renewable Energy Professional (REP)

Career Path

- Engineer → Project Manager → Energy Consultant → Director of Renewables

XVII
Entrepreneurship & Startup Roles

1. Idea Generation & Problem Validation

What They Do

- Identify real-world problems and brainstorm innovative solutions; validate the idea through research and customer feedback.

Skills to Build

- Market research, customer interviews
- Design thinking, lean startup methodology
- Business model canvas creation

Career Path

- Independent or within incubator/accelerator programs.

2. Startup Formation & Early Product Development

What They Do

- Legally form the startup; build a minimum viable product (MVP) to test the core idea quickly and inexpensively.

Skills to Build

- Basic coding or prototyping, project management
- Team formation and role assignment
- Legal basics: company registration, IP protection

Career Path

- Founders, co-founders, and initial team members.

3. Seed Funding & Market Testing

What They Do

- Raise initial capital from angel investors, friends, family, or seed funds; test the MVP with early customers.

Skills to Build

- Pitching and storytelling
- Financial planning and budgeting
- Customer acquisition and feedback analysis

Career Path

- Startup CEO and founding team actively engage with investors and customers.

4. Product-Market Fit & Customer Acquisition

What They Do

- Refine the product based on user feedback until it meets market demands; grow the customer base.

Skills to Build

- Data-driven decision making
- Digital marketing and growth hacking
- User experience (UX) and product management

Career Path

- Product managers, marketing leads join the team.

5. Scaling Operations & Team Building

What They Do

- Expand the team and operations to handle growing customer demand; optimize internal processes.

Skills to Build

- Leadership and people management
- Operational strategy, supply chain management
- HR and company culture development

Career Path

- Hiring C-suite executives, managers, and functional teams.

6. Series A/B Fundraising & Expansion

What They Do

- Secure larger investment rounds to scale technology, marketing, and sales; enter new markets.

Skills to Build

- Advanced fundraising and investor relations
- Strategic partnerships and alliances
- International business development

Career Path

- CEO and executive team focus on scaling and long-term strategy.

7. Exit Strategies & Serial Entrepreneurship

What They Do

- Plan for exit via acquisition, merger, or IPO; founders may start new ventures leveraging gained experience.

Skills to Build

- Negotiation and deal structuring
- IPO readiness and compliance
- Mentoring and ecosystem building

Career Path

- Successful founders become investors, advisors, or serial entrepreneurs.

Key Skills and Tools for Entrepreneurs & Startups:

- Lean Startup, Agile methodologies
- Financial modeling and budgeting tools (Excel, QuickBooks)
- Customer Relationship Management (CRM) software
- Digital marketing platforms (Google Ads, Facebook Ads)
- Project management tools (Trello, Asana, Jira)
- Pitch decks and storytelling

Recommended Certifications and Programs:

- Y Combinator Startup School
- Stanford Online Entrepreneurship Program
- Coursera / Udemy courses on startup fundamentals
- Local incubator/accelerator programs (Techstars, 500 Startups)

XVIII

Exposure – The Key to Clarity

You cannot become what you cannot see.

Exposure is the invisible force that transforms career confusion into clarity. You can read hundreds of books, attend lectures, and take online courses—but nothing substitutes real-world experience. The key difference between those who float through their careers and those who take charge is this: the depth of their exposure to reality. In this chapter, we'll break down what exposure really means, why it's essential, and practical, actionable ways to gain it.

Why Exposure Matters

Learn by Doing
Exposure places you in environments where you're not just absorbing information, but actively using it. It bridges the gap between textbook theory and on-the-ground reality.

See How Theory Applies in Real Life
What you study in school often feels abstract. Exposure lets you understand how those concepts are used in actual work scenarios—whether in design meetings, customer interactions, or R&D labs.

Build Meaningful Connections
Interacting with professionals gives you a glimpse into various roles and industries, and often leads to opportunities you didn't know existed.

Break Career Myths
You might think a certain role is boring or a field isn't lucrative until you actually see it firsthand.

Boost Your Confidence
Exposure helps you understand the norms, language, expectations, and pace of the industry, making you feel more prepared and confident.

Ways to Get Exposure

Let's now look at practical methods to build exposure across career paths:

1. Internships & Part-Time Jobs

What It Is:

- Temporary work arrangements (paid or unpaid) that give you hands-on experience in real work environments.

How It Helps:

- Understand industry culture
- Learn technical tools and workplace communication
- Build a portfolio of real-world projects

Pro Tip:
Start early—even during your first or second year of college. Every internship, even a small one, teaches something.

2. Volunteering in Real-World Projects

What It Is:

- Working on projects for NGOs, college fests, open-source platforms, or local businesses without expecting monetary rewards.

How It Helps:

- Gain team experience and leadership skills
- Build networks in non-traditional sectors
- Understand how to work with constraints and solve real problems

Examples:

- Volunteering at a tech fest and managing logistics
- Assisting in a rural development project
- Contributing code to an open-source app

3. Attending Conferences, Hackathons, and Webinars

What It Is:

- Events that bring together professionals, learners, and innovators for learning, showcasing, or problem-solving.

How It Helps:

- Discover industry trends and career paths
- Get feedback on your ideas from experts
- Compete or collaborate with people outside your circle

Pro Tip:
At every event, aim to talk to at least three people you didn't know before.
Those conversations can shape your direction.

4. Networking on LinkedIn

What It Is:

- An online platform to build professional connections, share your journey, and discover opportunities.

How It Helps:

- Connect with mentors, recruiters, founders
- Learn through others' journeys and insights
- Position yourself as a serious learner or young professional

Action Steps:

- Optimize your profile (photo, summary, skills)
- Engage with posts in your domain
- Send thoughtful connection requests—never just "Hi"

5. Shadowing Professionals

What It Is:

- Spending a day or a few hours observing a professional in their work environment.

How It Helps:

- Get an unfiltered view of what a job is really like
- Ask questions and understand their career journey

- Identify whether a role suits your temperament and interests

How to Do It:

- Reach out to family, alumni, or LinkedIn connections and politely ask if you can observe them for a few hours. It's one of the most underrated exposure techniques.

How Exposure Creates Career Clarity

Exposure takes you from "I think I want to do this" to "I've seen it and now I know." You begin to:

- Recognize your strengths and preferences based on experience, not assumptions.
- Rule out career paths that don't align with your energy, values, or aspirations.
- Identify skill gaps that you can then address through learning or practice.
- Build a personal brand through actual experiences rather than certifications alone.

Real Story:

Priya, a computer science undergrad, thought she wanted to work in app development. During her internship at a small fintech startup, she was exposed to product management and user research. She realized she was more excited about understanding customer problems than writing code. That exposure led her to pivot, take courses in UX, and now she's thriving as a product designer.

End-of-Chapter Activity

Ask yourself:

- Have I worked in at least 2 real-world settings?
- Have I interacted with professionals in my desired field?
- Have I attended at least one industry event or competition?
- Have I contributed to a project outside my college curriculum?
- Have I written or spoken publicly about what I learned?
- If not, now is the time.

XIX

Tools, Platforms, and Resources to Accelerate Your Career Journey

In a world of limitless choices, having the right tools is often more important than having more tools. Whether you're just starting, pivoting careers, or upskilling to stay relevant, this chapter lists the best platforms, apps, and resources to accelerate your career journey in a smart and structured way.

Self-Discovery & Career Planning Tools

Before setting out on a career path, it's vital to understand your strengths, personality, interests, and values. These tools help with introspection and goal alignment:

16Personalities.com:
Based on the MBTI framework, helps you understand your behavior, preferences, and potential work environments.

Mindler:
Career assessment and guidance platform, especially useful for Indian students, offering personalized career paths.

CareerExplorer:
Provides detailed personality and career assessments, matching you with suitable fields.

Ikigai Worksheets:
Simple yet profound tool to identify your "reason for being" — the intersection of what you love, what you're good at, what the world needs, and what you can be paid for.

Trello / Notion / Asana:
Visual platforms for goal setting, tracking progress, and planning your career roadmap.

MindMeister / XMind:
For mind mapping ideas, visualizing skills and interests.

Learning Platforms – Acquire In-Demand Skills

The key to career growth is lifelong learning. Whether it's technical skills, creative mastery, or communication, these platforms provide expert-led learning:

Coursera / edX / Khan Academy:
University-grade courses across disciplines with certifications.

Udemy:
Affordable, practical courses ranging from business to programming to design.

Skillshare:
Ideal for creatives and hobbyists – from photography and design to branding and productivity.

LinkedIn Learning:
Bite-sized lessons aligned with professional skills and workplace readiness.

Building Your Portfolio – Showcase What You Can Do

In today's digital-first world, having a portfolio is as important as a resume. These platforms help you build and showcase your work:

GitHub:
For coders, programmers, and open-source contributors – a must-have to demonstrate coding projects.

Behance:
For graphic designers, UI/UX designers, and creatives to display portfolios professionally.

Medium:
For writers, bloggers, and thought leaders to share ideas, insights, and build an audience.

Notion / Carrd / Wix / WordPress:
Build personal websites or resume sites without needing to code.

Industry Exposure & Networking Platforms

Networking isn't just about finding jobs — it's about learning, gaining visibility, and joining professional circles:

LinkedIn:
Still the most powerful tool for building a professional brand, following companies, and connecting with mentors.

Shapr:
Often called "Tinder for professional networking" — swipe to match with professionals who share your goals.

Twitter / X:
Great for following industry leaders, especially in tech, startups, and media. Build visibility by engaging in meaningful threads.

Discord Communities:
Many tech, design, and gaming communities thrive on Discord. Engage in channels that align with your career.

Meetup / Eventbrite:
Find virtual and offline events to learn and network with peers and experts.

Internships & Real-World Exposure Platforms

Hands-on experience is critical, especially in the early stages. These platforms help you find internships, freelance gigs, and remote jobs:

Internshala / LetsIntern:
Internship search engines with filters by field, location, and stipend — great for students and freshers.

AngelList (Wellfound):
Find roles in early-stage startups across tech, design, marketing, etc.

Turing:
A platform for remote software engineering jobs with global companies.

Jobspikr:
Aggregates real-time job and internship listings from around the world, including hidden opportunities.

Job Preparation & Practice Platforms

These tools help you practice and prepare for competitive job roles, especially in tech:

LeetCode / HackerRank / InterviewBit:
Essential platforms for practicing coding, data structures, algorithms, and mock interviews — especially useful for software/tech jobs.

Resume.io / Canva:
Easily design beautiful, ATS-friendly resumes and cover letters, even with zero design background.

Glassdoor / AmbitionBox:
Research company reviews, salaries, and interview experiences to prepare strategically.

Productivity & Personal Growth Tools

Smart professionals manage their time, energy, and mindset. These tools help build discipline and clarity:

Forest / Focus To-Do / Pomofocus:
Use Pomodoro timers to stay focused while studying or working.

Evernote / OneNote:
Digital notebooks for organizing research, thoughts, ideas, and lecture notes.

Headspace / Calm / Insight Timer:
Meditation and mindfulness apps to reduce burnout and increase emotional resilience.

Entrepreneurship & Startup Resources

If you're inclined toward creating your own business or launching a startup, these are your go-to tools:

Y Combinator's Startup School:
Free structured startup curriculum from the world's top accelerator.

Startup Grind:
Global community for networking, mentorship, and startup stories.

Crunchbase:
Explore data on startups, funding, and investor activity.

Stripe Atlas / Firstbase.io:
Tools to help legally incorporate your startup globally.

Research & Academia Platforms

Planning to pursue higher studies, publish papers, or engage in academic research? These tools support scholarly growth:

Google Scholar:
Academic search engine to find credible research papers.

ResearchGate / Academia.edu:
Collaborate with researchers, share your work, and access academic content.

Zotero / Mendeley:
Reference managers for organizing papers and auto-generating citations.

Career Assessments & Personality Tests

Knowing yourself is the foundation of career clarity:

MBTI / 16Personalities.com:
Comprehensive personality assessments to understand communication and decision-making styles.

Holland Code / RIASEC Test:
Matches personality with career environments (Realistic, Investigative, Artistic, etc.).

StrengthsFinder (CliftonStrengths):
Helps identify and apply your top personal strengths.

Summary

Build Your Career Toolbox Intentionally. Choosing the right tools empowers you to:

- Plan your career path confidently
- Learn new skills with focus
- Present your work professionally
- Prepare strategically for jobs and interviews
- Connect meaningfully with your industry
- Manage your personal growth holistically

Your journey becomes more efficient and impactful when you learn to use tools not as crutches, but as levers.

XX
Mindset & Soft Skills – The Real Differentiators

In a world where automation and AI can replace hard skills quickly, what remains irreplaceable is the human touch. Employers no longer hire just for degrees — they hire for how you think, how you collaborate, how you handle change, and how you lead. This chapter uncovers the essential mindset and soft skills that make you stand out — not just in interviews, but across your entire career.

Skills You Must Master

Let's explore six foundational soft skills and habits that act as multipliers for all your technical knowledge.

1. Communication – Writing & Speaking

"The art of communication is the language of leadership." – James Humes

No matter your role or industry, you need to express thoughts clearly — in person, on paper, and on digital platforms.

- Mastering Writing: Learn to write structured emails, proposals, reports, and summaries. Practice journaling to improve clarity of thought. Use tools like Grammarly or Hemingway Editor to polish your writing.
- Improving Speaking: Practice articulation and voice modulation. Record yourself to understand tone and pacing. Participate in clubs like Toastmasters or local debate groups.

Pro tip: Communication isn't just about talking — it's about listening with intention.

2. Critical Thinking & Problem Solving

"Don't bring me problems. Bring me solutions." – Every great manager ever

Companies don't pay you just to follow instructions — they value those who can analyze, question, and create better ways to solve problems.
How to build it:

- Practice breaking down problems using the 5 Whys or Root Cause Analysis.
- Develop structured thinking using mind maps or frameworks like SWOT.
- Read case studies, solve real-world problems, and learn basic logic puzzles.

Application Example: Whether you're a coder fixing a bug, a marketer analyzing campaign results, or a product designer building features, problem-solving is your biggest asset.

3. Adaptability & Resilience

"It is not the strongest or the most intelligent who will survive but those who can best manage change." – Charles Darwin

Change is constant. The real skill? Learning how to stay calm, assess the situation, and adapt fast.
How to develop it:

- Reflect regularly: Ask yourself, "What did I learn from this experience?"

- Embrace failure as feedback, not a full stop.
- Stay open to re-learning — even if it means letting go of past expertise.

Mini-practice: Try doing things outside your comfort zone once a week — public speaking, a cold email, a coding challenge, or learning a new language.

4. Teamwork & Leadership

"If you want to go fast, go alone. If you want to go far, go together." – African Proverb

Even in highly individual roles, collaboration is key. Leadership isn't just for managers — it's about taking ownership and inspiring others, regardless of your title.

Build teamwork by:

- Practicing empathy and active listening.
- Giving and receiving feedback constructively.
- Taking initiative even when it's not "your job."

Grow leadership by:

- Volunteering to lead a project or event.
- Mentoring a junior peer.
- Making decisions and owning their outcomes.
- Mindset: Leadership is about influence, not authority.

5. Digital Literacy

"Being literate in today's world means being fluent in the digital language of tools, data, and online behavior."

Whether you're a teacher, an engineer, or a founder — digital literacy is non-negotiable.

What it means:

- Understanding how to use collaborative tools (Google Suite, Zoom, Trello, Slack).
- Navigating digital research and online security basics.
- Knowing your way around basic data interpretation (spreadsheets, dashboards).

Stay up to date with:

- New apps, AI tools, and platforms relevant to your field.
- Keyboard shortcuts, browser extensions, and productivity hacks.

Tip: The faster you learn new tools, the more valuable you become to any team.

Mindset Shifts to Cultivate

Your mindset — how you think, perceive, and react — often determines how far you go. Here are some powerful mindset shifts that every young professional must make:

Shift 1: From "What should I do?" → "What am I curious about?"

Instead of asking the world what career to choose, start by asking yourself:

- What am I naturally curious about?
- What tasks make me lose track of time?
- What problems do I enjoy solving, even if I'm not the best at them yet?

Curiosity leads to learning. Learning leads to mastery. Mastery leads to opportunity.

Shift 2: From "I need a job" → "I want to build a career"

A job is short-term. A career is a journey. Think long-term:

- What do you want to be known for in 10 years?
- What skills can compound over time?
- What industries excite you beyond the salary?
- When you stop chasing just a paycheck, you start crafting a legacy.

Shift 3: From "I'm not good at this" → "I'm not good at this yet"

- The power of a growth mindset means believing skills are built, not born.
- View mistakes as part of the process.
- Praise effort and improvement, not just outcomes.
- Set learning goals, not just performance goals.

Example: Don't say, "I'm bad at public speaking." Say, "I'm practicing public speaking to get better."

Shift 4: From "I work hard" → "I work smart & with purpose"

- Effort is great. But alignment matters more.
- Learn to prioritize using the Eisenhower Matrix (urgent vs important).
- Focus on high-leverage activities — those that produce long-term results.
- Work with intention, not just on tasks.

How to Practice Soft Skills Consistently

- Join student groups, clubs, or online communities.
- Practice leadership, communication, and teamwork in low-stakes environments.
- Volunteer for roles or internships where soft skills are required.
- Even unpaid projects can sharpen real-world capabilities.
- Keep a feedback journal.

- After presentations, group work, or meetings, ask for feedback and write down what you learned.
- Record yourself.
- Whether you're practicing interviews, pitches, or presentations — watching yourself helps refine delivery.
- Conclusion: Be the Human AI Can't Replace

Soft skills + strong mindset = career differentiator.

You can learn Python or marketing or UI/UX. But what makes you irreplaceable is how you think, lead, adapt, communicate, and solve problems — across every phase of your journey. As technology advances, your mindset and soft skills are what ensure you thrive, not just survive.

End-of-Chapter Activity

Rate yourself on a scale of 1 (Needs Work) to 5 (Strong Skill) for the following:

- Written communication
- Verbal communication
- Problem-solving ability
- Critical thinking
- Adaptability to change
- Resilience after failure
- Team collaboration
- Leadership/Initiative-taking
- Digital tool proficiency

Action: Identify your top strengths and areas for improvement. Write & execute ways to further develop each weak area.

XXI

Education Options After Each Stage

After Class 10ᵗʰ (Generally age 15–16; foundation for future specialization)

1. Choose Academic Stream (Class 11–12):

- Science (PCM/PCB): Ideal for engineering, medicine, research
- Commerce: Business, accounting, finance, management
- Arts/Humanities: Social sciences, media, law, design, civil services

2. Skill-based/Diploma Courses (if not continuing regular school):

- Polytechnic Diplomas (Engineering, IT, Architecture)
- ITI (Industrial Training Institute) certifications (Electrician, Fitter, Mechanic, etc.)
- Certificate programs in graphic design, animation, web development, hospitality

3. Open Schooling / NIOS:

- For those needing flexible learning due to personal circumstances or skill-building priorities

After Diploma (Generally a 3-year program after Class 10)

1. Lateral Entry to Engineering (B.Tech/B.E.):

- Direct admission into 2nd year of UG engineering
- Fields: Mechanical, Civil, Computer Science, Electrical, etc.

2. Professional Certifications:

- AWS, Cisco, CompTIA (for IT)
- CAD, CAM tools (for Mechanical/Architecture)

3. Specialized Bachelor Programs:

- BCA, BBA, B.Sc. IT, Design programs, depending on interest

4. Apprenticeship + Skill Advancement:

- Work-study models in industries like manufacturing, telecom, construction

After Class 12th (The critical branching point; generally age 17–18)

1. Undergraduate Degrees (3–5 years):

- B.Sc., B.A., B.Com. – General degree programs
- B.Tech./B.E. – Engineering
- MBBS, BDS, BAMS, BHMS – Medical fields
- BBA, BBM – Management
- BCA – Computer Applications
- B.Des., BFA, B.Arch. – Design, Art, Architecture
- LLB (integrated) – Law (BA+LLB)

2. Vocational/Skill Programs:

- Hotel Management
- Animation and VFX
- Culinary Arts
- Event Management
- Photography
- Sports Management

3. Competitive Exams for Government Jobs:

- NDA (Defence)
- SSC CHSL
- State-level exams for clerical/technical roles

After Undergraduate (UG) (Usually 3–4 years of college, age 21–22)

1. Postgraduate Degrees (1–2 years):

- M.A., M.Sc., M.Com. – For specialization in arts/sciences/commerce
- MBA, M.Tech, MCA – Professional qualifications
- MS (Abroad) – For deeper subject expertise, especially in STEM
- Integrated PhD – For research-focused students

2. Government Exams:

- UPSC Civil Services
- State PSC, SSC CGL, Banking (IBPS, SBI)
- Railways, Defence, Teaching (TET, NET)

3. Professional Certifications:

- CFA, CA, CS, ACCA (Finance)
- PMP, Six Sigma (Management)
- Data Analytics, Cybersecurity, AI/ML (Tech)

4. Work + Upskill:

- Work in industry while pursuing part-time PG, online courses, or micro-degrees

After Postgraduate (PG) (Usually age 23–25+)

1. PhD / Doctoral Programs:

- In your subject of expertise (Humanities, Sciences, Engineering, Social Sciences)
- Entrance via NET (India), GRE (abroad), GATE (tech/research)
- Leads to academic, research, think tank, and R&D careers

2. Professional and Executive Programs:

- Executive MBA (IIMs, ISB, etc.)
- Fellowships (e.g., Young India Fellowship, Teach for India)
- Leadership programs (e.g., World Economic Forum Global Shapers)

3. Specialized Diplomas / Certifications:

- Niche skills like UX Design, Data Science, Policy Making, and Entrepreneurship

4. Startups / Consulting / NGOs / Global Jobs:

- Apply education in social impact, innovation, or international opportunities

After PhD (Final formal academic tier; typically age 28+)

• 128 •

Postdoctoral Research:

- Academic research fellowships in India or abroad (IITs, Harvard, Max Planck, etc.)

XXII

Job Options After Each Education Level

After Class 10th (Entry-level, skill-based, or apprenticeship roles)

Government/Defense Roles:

- Indian Army (as Soldier GD, Tradesman, Technical)
- Police Constable (state-level exams)
- Railways Group D posts
- SSC MTS (Multi-Tasking Staff)

Private Sector Jobs:

- Retail Associate / Salesperson
- Office Assistant / Clerk / Data Entry Operator
- Delivery Executive (e.g., Amazon, Flipkart)
- Call Center Executive
- Field Technician (with ITI skill)

- Helper roles in manufacturing and logistics

Apprenticeships:

- Under National Apprenticeship Promotion Scheme (NAPS)
- PSU apprentice trainee roles (Railways, BHEL, HAL)

After Diploma (usually in engineering or technical fields)

Technical & Skilled Jobs:

- Junior Engineer (JE) in Railways, PWD, CPWD, etc.
- Technician roles in telecom, manufacturing, construction
- CAD Draftsman / Civil Site Supervisor
- Assistant Technician (Electrical, Mechanical, Automobile)
- IT support staff/hardware technician

Private Sector Jobs:

- Maintenance Engineer
- CNC Machine Operator
- BPO / KPO jobs
- Graphic Designer (if studied design tools)
- Field Service Engineer (electronics/mechatronics)

Government Jobs:

- SSC JE
- State JE/Technician level jobs

- PSU Trainee roles (IOCL, NTPC, SAIL, etc.)

After Class 12th

Government Sector:

- SSC CHSL (Clerk, DEO, LDC)
- Indian Army/Navy/Airforce (as Technical Entry / Clerk / Tradesman)
- Police Constable / Fire Services
- Railways Group C/D jobs
- Banking assistant roles (via IBPS Clerk after 12th in some states)

Private Sector:

- Customer Support / Call Center Executive
- Digital Marketing Assistant
- Junior Graphic Designer
- Content Creator (for YouTube, blogging, social media)
- Social Media Manager (entry-level for small brands)
- Data Entry / Back Office Executive

Freelance / Self-employment:

- Home tutor
- YouTuber / Influencer
- Dropshipping or affiliate marketing

After Undergraduate (UG)

Core Job Profiles:

- Engineering Grads: Software Developer, Network Engineer, QA Tester, Design Engineer
- Commerce Grads: Accountant, Financial Analyst, Tax Assistant, Bank PO
- Science Grads: Lab Technician, Research Assistant, Pharma Sales, School Teacher
- Arts Grads: Content Writer, HR Executive, Digital Marketer, Civil Services Aspirant

Competitive Exams:

- UPSC (IAS, IPS, IFS)
- State PSC Exams
- SSC CGL
- Banking (IBPS PO, SBI PO)
- Railway NTPC
- LIC/GIC AAO

Entrepreneurship / Startups:

- Start your own brand, app, or service
- Freelancer (coding, writing, photography, design)

After Postgraduate (PG)

Advanced Roles:

- MBA Grads: Business Analyst, Product Manager, Marketing Manager, Operations Head
- M.Tech: Research & Development, Senior Software Engineer, AI/ML Engineer
- MCA: App Developer, IT Consultant, System Architect
- MA/MSc: Policy Analyst, Researcher, Psychologist, Content Strategist

Government Jobs:

- UPSC, State PSC (if not done earlier)
- Assistant Professor (with UGC NET)
- Higher administrative roles in government or PSUs

Specialized Private Sector Roles:

- Consulting (McKinsey, Deloitte, etc.)
- Policy Fellowships (e.g., LAMP, Gandhi Fellowship)
- Corporate Training & L&D

Global Opportunities:

- Apply for jobs abroad in tech, business, design, and education

After PhD

Academia & Research:

- Assistant/Associate Professor
- University Researcher
- Head of Department (later)

Industry Research & Strategy:

- R&D Labs (Tech, Pharma, Biotech, Engineering)
- Research Lead / Data Scientist (Tech)
- Corporate Strategy roles

Public Policy & Think Tanks:

- Policy Analyst
- Research Fellow (NITI Aayog, Brookings, UNESCO, etc.)

Entrepreneurship / Thought Leadership:

- Author, Speaker, Consultant
- Start a niche knowledge-based venture

XXIII

Real Stories of Career Transitions

From Stuck to Steered – Non-Linear Paths That Inspire

In a world that's changing faster than curricula, job titles, and even industry lifespans, linear careers are becoming obsolete. The most successful and fulfilled professionals often walk paths no one expected, including themselves. This chapter shares five real-world-inspired stories that serve as a beacon for anyone feeling "stuck" or "unsure".

1. Engineer to Product Designer – The Bridge Between Tech and Empathy

Name: Priya R.
Background: B.Tech in Mechanical Engineering
Current Role: UX/Product Designer at a FinTech Startup

Story:
Priya was always good at math and building models, which made engineering an obvious choice. But deep down, she was fascinated by psychology and art. During her final year, she joined a hackathon, and instead of writing code, she started sketching interfaces. That sparked a journey into UI/UX. She completed online certifications from Coursera and

DesignLab, built a portfolio using Figma and Adobe XD, and landed her first freelance gig through LinkedIn. Her technical background became a superpower — she could talk to engineers and design for users.

Lesson:
You don't need to abandon your technical degree to be creative. You just need to find the intersection between what you studied and what you love.

2. Teacher to EdTech Entrepreneur – Turning Frustration into Innovation

Name: Manish K.
Background: Secondary School Teacher
Current Role: Founder, LearnWisely – a digital classroom tool for Tier-2 schools

Story:
Manish taught math in a rural school for 8 years. He saw firsthand how a lack of tech access and poor engagement were failing students. Frustrated, he began designing worksheets on Canva, created short explainer videos on YouTube, and experimented with Google Forms for assessments. This hobby turned into a startup idea. He joined a local incubator, pitched to investors, and within 2 years had 100+ schools onboard. His startup didn't just digitize learning — it solved real, local problems teachers face.

Lesson:
You don't need to quit your job to start something. Sometimes your pain points become your product.

3. College Dropout to AI Consultant – Learning Beyond the Syllabus

Name: Aditya J.
Background: Dropped out of B.Sc Computer Science after the 2nd year
Current Role: AI Consultant for MNCs in India & Europe

Story:
Aditya felt unchallenged by the rigid education system. While his friends

were stuck in theory, he was building Python projects and taking deep learning courses from Stanford (online). He contributed to open-source GitHub repos, answered ML questions on Stack Overflow, and started a blog explaining AI concepts in simple language. A blog post he wrote went viral. A European startup reached out. That was the start of his freelance consulting career. Today, he works remotely, helps build AI models, and mentors young learners.

Lesson:
Credentials matter less than evidence of skill. Build. Share. Teach. And doors will open.

4. Small Town Student to Leading Space Research Center Intern – From Stargazing to Space Missions

Name: Ahmed
Background: B.Sc Physics from a small-town university
Current Role: Intern at a Leading Space Research Center

Story:
Ahmed grew up in a quiet town where even internet access arrived late. But what he always had was a head full of questions about the stars. Without formal coaching or facilities, he taught himself the basics of astrophysics using borrowed books and community resources. Determined to learn more, he even built a working telescope from discarded materials and co-authored a research paper with guidance from a retired professor. His first attempt to get into an international space internship program didn't work out. But he didn't stop. Ahmed joined global science camps, added hands-on projects to his portfolio, and tried again. This time, he got in. Now, he's working at one of the world's top space research centers—bringing small-town dreams to life and inspiring other students across rural India to chase theirs.

Lesson:
Access can be limited. Ambition shouldn't be. Keep applying. Keep learning. Keep dreaming.

5. Commerce Student to Ethical Hacker – Cracking Codes, Not Just Numbers

Name: Sameer N.
Background: B.Com Graduate
Current Role: Certified Ethical Hacker & Cybersecurity Analyst

Story:
Sameer always had a knack for puzzles and computers, but chose commerce due to parental pressure. During lockdown, he stumbled upon a cybersecurity YouTube channel and started learning how ethical hacking works. He completed certifications like CEH (Certified Ethical Hacker), OSCP, and practiced in labs. With an unconventional background, he faced skepticism — until he hacked a dummy system during an interview, proving his skills. Now, he works with banks to test their cybersecurity systems.

Lesson:
Your degree doesn't define your destiny. Passion, practice, and persistence do.

Final Reflection: What These Stories Teach Us

Non-linear ≠ wrong. It's often the most powerful path. Each of these individuals used curiosity, persistence, and self-learning to create their playbook. Success is no longer tied to marks, degrees, or big-city backgrounds — but to initiative, problem-solving, and the courage to try.

End-of-Chapter Activity

- Go online and find one person in your dream field whose journey was non-traditional (e.g., on LinkedIn, YouTube, Medium).
- Read or watch their story.
- Note the unexpected twists or decisions they made.
- Summarize in a few sentences what made their career path unique and what you can learn from it.

XXIV
Action Plan for Readers

Your 30-Day Career Clarity Challenge

"Clarity doesn't come from overthinking. It comes from action."

All the awareness, insights, tools, and stories you've explored in this book will only be useful if you take the next step. Not a giant leap. Just consistent, focused steps — week by week. That's why we've created the 30-Day Career Clarity Challenge, a simple but powerful month-long journey that takes you from confusion to direction. Each week has a clear theme, daily micro-tasks, and reflection prompts to ensure you don't just learn — you evolve.

Week 1: Know Yourself – Self-Assessment + Career Interests

This is your foundation. Before you build a skyscraper, you must know the ground you're building on — your values, strengths, interests, and motivators.

Goals:

- Discover what energizes or drains you
- Identify your top career interest areas

Daily Actions:

- Day 1: Take a self-assessment (16Personalities.com or Mindler)
- Day 2: Journal your past wins and what you enjoyed about them
- Day 3: Do an Ikigai worksheet – What you love, what you're good at, what the world needs, what you can be paid for
- Day 4: Take a career interests quiz (CareerExplorer.com)
- Day 5: Ask 3 friends/family: "What's one thing I'm naturally good at?"
- Day 6: Write your top 3 career values (e.g., creativity, impact, stability)
- Day 7: Reflect: What patterns are emerging? What excites you?

Week 2: Explore Opportunities – Dive into 3 Industries

Curiosity is your superpower. Instead of feeling like you need to "decide your future," act like a career detective and explore.

Goals:

- Learn about real roles and industries
- Compare pros and cons, growth potential, and entry paths

Daily Actions:

- Day 8: Choose 3 industries you're curious about (e.g., AI, Design, EdTech)
- Day 9: Watch a YouTube Day-in-the-Life video for each industry
- Day 10: Read 1 article from each industry's leading publication
- Day 11: Browse job roles on LinkedIn or Naukri in those industries
- Day 12: List the top 3 skills needed in each
- Day 13: Research career roadmaps and educational paths
- Day 14: Reflect: Which one excites you most and why?

Week 3: Connect & Learn – Talk to People + Attend 1 Event

Career clarity accelerates through conversations, not just introspection. Learning from others' real stories and advice is invaluable.

Goals:

- Expand your network
- Learn from real-world professionals
- Build confidence in outreach

Daily Actions:

- Day 15: Create or update your LinkedIn profile (if not already)
- Day 16: Write a short "curious learner" message template
- Day 17: Identify and follow 5 professionals from industries you explored
- Day 18: Send personalized messages to them (e.g., "I'm a student curious about your field. Could I ask a few questions?")
- Day 19: Prepare 3 smart questions to ask in an informational chat
- Day 20: Attend 1 online webinar, community meetup, or career fair (Eventbrite, Discord, LinkedIn Events, etc.)
- Day 21: Reflect: What insights did you gain from these conversations?

Week 4: Build & Begin – LinkedIn, Portfolio, and Passion Project

Now it's time to take initiative and build something that reflects your interest. This could be small — a blog post, a video, a design, or a case study. Just start.

Goals:

- Build visibility for your work and potential
- Gain early momentum toward your chosen career field

Daily Actions:

- Day 22: Optimize your LinkedIn "About" section using your Self-Discovery report
- Day 23: Upload any certificates or add relevant skills
- Day 24: Publish your first post on something you learned (reflection, industry insight, etc.)
- Day 25: Choose a small 7-day project in your area of interest (e.g., code a tool, design a poster, write a guide, etc.)
- Day 26–28: Execute your project in micro steps
- Day 29: Share your mini project online (LinkedIn, GitHub, Behance, etc.)
- Day 30: Reflect: What did this project teach you about your passion and potential?

What Happens After the 30 Days?

- You'll have a clearer sense of direction, not just theory
- You'll know your strengths, interests, and real-world role models
- You'll have built credibility, connections, and momentum
- And most importantly, you'll be in motion — learning by doing

End-of-Chapter Activity

Write a personal commitment statement summarizing your career goal or focus area, including:. What you are committed to learning or exploring. How often you will dedicate time to your career development. Your motivation behind this commitment.

XXV

Diagnostic Questions for Schools, Teachers, Parents, and Students Claiming Innovation and Future-Readiness

Academic and Intellectual Exposure

- How many students have:

  - Participated in national or international STEM conferences?
  - Been selected for academic exchanges or research summits?
  - Published original work — books, papers, or articles?

Innovation, Creativity & Prototyping

- How many students have:

  - Built working prototypes or tech solutions?
  - Participated in or won hackathons or science fairs?
  - Applied to AIM, Inspire Awards – MANAK, or similar platforms?

Awards & Recognitions

- Has your school produced students who received:

  - Rashtriya Bal Puraskar?
  - James Dyson Award, Google Science Fair, or Intel ISEF?
  - National or international innovation and leadership awards?

Career Diversity

- Can you share data on alumni who are now in:

  - Entrepreneurship
  - Design, Arts, and Media
  - Social Impact, Policy, Literature, or Sports
  - Any domain beyond engineering and medicine?

Real-World Preparedness

- How many students:

  - Have done internships, apprenticeships, or community projects?
  - Attended career mentoring with real-world professionals?
  - Experienced a structured goal-setting and tracking system in school?

If you cannot confidently answer these, your school may have a gap between ambition and execution.

XXVI

A Message to Students: You Are the Driver of Your Journey

Dear Student,

You don't need to have it all figured out right now. The world might be moving fast. People around you might seem sure of what they want. But here's the truth: most people are still figuring it out—just like you. And that's okay. What matters is this: you're willing to explore, reflect, and take action. That mindset alone puts you on the path to something meaningful. Your career is not just a job—it's your way of creating value in the world while living a life that feels right for you. It should reflect your strengths, your interests, and the kind of impact you want to make. It won't be a straight path, and it won't come with a perfect map. But if you learn how to steer—with clarity, curiosity, and courage—you'll go further than you imagine.

Here's what to keep in mind as you begin your journey:

Start with yourself
Understand who you are. Your values, your strengths, the things that excite or frustrate you—these are signals pointing toward the life you want to build. Pay attention.

Try things early and often
Don't wait to be "ready." Start now. Volunteer. Intern. Build. Shadow someone. Launch a project. Each step teaches you something—about work, about people, and about yourself.

Don't chase someone else's dream
Just because a path is popular or profitable doesn't mean it's right for you. Success means little without fulfillment. Be bold enough to define success on your own terms.

Use technology to your advantage
The tools to learn anything and connect with anyone are already in your hands. Use them. Learn new skills online. Follow creators who inspire you. Share your ideas. Build your personal brand.

You are allowed to change
Don't be afraid to pivot. What you choose today isn't set in stone. You will grow, evolve, and find new callings. The world changes. So can you.

Ask for help
You are not alone in this. Teachers, mentors, family members—many want to support you. Reach out. Ask questions. Listen and learn.

Define your own version of "real success"
Maybe it's building a business, maybe it's writing a book, maybe it's leading a team, maybe it's helping your community. There is no single path. But there is your path.

This book, Steer, was written to help you ask better questions, discover real opportunities, and take ownership of your future. Not just to land a job—but to live a life of intention and impact. So take the wheel. You may not know your destination yet, but you're more ready than you think to begin the journey.

XXVII

A Message to Parents: From Control to Connection

As parents, you are the most influential force in your child's life. You shape their earliest beliefs—about themselves, about success, and about what's possible. But in a world that's evolving faster than ever, our approach to guiding children must evolve too. Gone are the days when career paths were linear, predictable, and bound by a few safe choices. Today, new industries emerge every year, and lifelong careers may take on many forms: corporate roles, freelancing, entrepreneurship, research, social innovation, and even careers that don't exist yet. In this new reality, our children don't need rigid instructions—they need open conversations. They don't need us to chart their future—they need us to walk alongside them as they discover it.

Here's how you can support this journey:

- Shift from answers to questions. Instead of saying, "You should be a doctor," ask, "What kind of problems excite you? What are you curious about?"
- Embrace exploration. Let your child try internships, side projects, new skills—even if it feels uncertain. Exploration leads to clarity.
- Resist comparison. Every child is on a unique timeline. Their success is not a race, and it's not measured by how quickly they fit into society's

boxes.
- Be a mirror, not a map. Reflect your child's strengths and passions back to them. Affirm who they are, not who you wish they'd become.
- Support reflection and resilience. Teach them that failure, doubt, and change are natural parts of growth—not signs of weakness.
- Most importantly, recognize that your love, presence, and belief in them are far more valuable than any career advice.

This book, Steer, was written to help young people find clarity and confidence—but also to remind parents that career guidance is not just about professions, it's about identity, purpose, and potential. Let's raise not just successful children—but fulfilled, self-aware, and courageous adults.

XXVIII

A Message to Teachers: Beyond the Classroom Walls

Dear Teachers,

You are more than educators—you are architects of possibility. Every day, in ways both visible and subtle, you shape the future. You introduce young people not just to concepts and content, but to confidence, curiosity, and self-belief. And yet, in the rush to complete syllabi, prepare for exams, and manage classrooms, one essential mission often gets sidelined: preparing students for life beyond school. In a world that no longer guarantees linear careers or lifelong job security, students need more than academic excellence. They need clarity of direction, exposure to the real world, and the mindset to adapt and grow. And this is where your role evolves—from instructor to mentor, from curriculum guide to career catalyst.

Here's how you can help students steer toward their future:

- Create space for exploration. Encourage questions that go beyond the textbook. Let students wonder aloud: What excites me? What kind of problems do I want to solve?
- Embed career context into your teaching. Whether it's physics or literature, draw connections to real-world applications and industries.

Help students see that what they're learning has a future use.

- Model lifelong learning. Share your own journey of learning and adapting. Let students see that even adults are still growing, still figuring things out.
- Celebrate diverse talents. Not every student will shine on tests. Some are artists, some are tinkerers, some are leaders. Your recognition may be the first affirmation of their unique potential.
- Be a guide, not just a grader. Have conversations about life, values, and aspirations. A single comment from you could spark a lifelong pursuit in a student.
- Collaborate with the world outside. Invite guest speakers. Encourage live projects. Facilitate industry exposure. Help students meet the world before they have to face it alone.

As we prepare students for an uncertain and rapidly changing world, your influence becomes more crucial than ever. You have the power not just to teach, but to ignite. This book, Steer, is as much a guide for students as it is a call to educators—to reimagine schooling not just as a path to exams, but as a launchpad for purpose. Thank you for your tireless work, your quiet impact, and your belief in the potential of every learner.

XXIX

A Message to Schools: From Teaching to Transforming Futures

Schools have always held the power to shape lives. They are the places where young minds are introduced to knowledge, values, and the social fabric of society. Yet, as the world changes rapidly—through technology, economic shifts, climate concerns, and evolving career landscapes—the role of schools must evolve too. Too often, education is reduced to exam scores and grade-level achievements. But the true purpose of schooling is not just to teach, but to prepare. To prepare students not just for tests, but for life. For work. For identity. For contribution. It's time we integrate career readiness, goal clarity, and real-world learning into the school experience. This doesn't mean abandoning academics, but enriching them. It means:

- Helping students understand their unique strengths, interests, and values
- Exposing them to diverse industries, professions, and future pathways
- Teaching them how to set meaningful goals, make informed choices, and adapt to change
- Providing access to mentors, projects, and practical experiences that go beyond textbooks
- Career education should not be an afterthought—it should be a foundational pillar, starting as early as middle school and building

through high school.

When schools embrace this shift, they don't just produce high-achievers—they cultivate purpose-driven, self-aware, future-ready individuals who know how to navigate uncertainty, collaborate across domains, and build lives that matter to them and the world. This book, Steer, is a call to action. It's a resource for students, but also for educators, principals, curriculum designers, and school leaders who care deeply about preparing the next generation—not for the past, but for the future. Let this be the decade when schools become launchpads, not just classrooms.

XXX

A Message to Policy Makers: Laying the Groundwork for Future-Ready Education

Dear Policy Makers,

The future of our workforce—and our society—sits in our classrooms today. As stewards of national development, you play a pivotal role in shaping the educational systems that influence how millions of young people think, learn, and prepare for life. For too long, however, our school systems have focused narrowly on academic performance and standardized exams, leaving students underprepared for the complex, dynamic world of work. In this era of automation, AI, and rapid industry transformation, career readiness is no longer a luxury—it is a necessity. We must equip students not only with information, but with direction, adaptability, and the confidence to navigate change. This requires systemic reform. And that begins with you.

Here's how policy can bridge the gap between school and the real world:

Mandate career readiness as a core component of curriculum
Introduce structured career education from middle school onwards.

Scaffold it across grade levels with age-appropriate modules on self-discovery, industry exposure, goal setting, and life planning.

Support experiential learning opportunities
Fund programs that enable internships, project-based learning, mentorships, and workplace exposure. Learning should extend beyond textbooks into companies, NGOs, and communities.

Incentivize industry-school partnerships
Provide tax benefits or grants to organizations that collaborate with schools to offer career talks, real-world projects, site visits, or mentorships.

Invest in teacher retooling
Equip educators with the training and tools they need to serve as career mentors—not just content instructors. Professional development should include industry trends, career coaching basics, and reflective facilitation skills.

Prioritize equity in access
Ensure that students in rural and under-resourced areas also receive career guidance, exposure, and opportunity—not just those in elite urban schools.

Champion lifelong learning frameworks
Encourage policies that support skill stacking, continuous upskilling, and vocational flexibility. The future will reward adaptability more than rigid expertise.

Career education isn't a separate add-on to school—it is the very purpose of it. Education must prepare young people for life, not just for exams. With the right policies, we can close the widening gap between classroom knowledge and career clarity. This is your moment to future-proof an entire generation—not just for employment, but for purpose-driven, resilient, and meaningful work.

CONCLUSION: YOUR JOURNEY FORWARD

Congratulations on completing Steer: A Real-World Guide to Career Clarity and Change. By investing time and energy into this process, you have taken the most important step toward shaping a career—and a life—that truly aligns with who you are and who you want to become.

In this age of rapid technological transformation, career paths are no longer linear or predictable. The future belongs to those who adapt, learn continuously, and courageously explore new possibilities. You now understand that clarity is not a fixed destination but an ongoing journey—one fueled by curiosity, deliberate action, and reflection. You've learned how to uncover your strengths, passions, and values. You've explored diverse industries, connected with professionals, and developed practical skills that set you apart. Most importantly, you've built a mindset that embraces change, challenges limiting beliefs, and views setbacks as stepping stones. Remember, no one else can steer your career better than you. Your unique combination of talents, experiences, and dreams is your compass. Trust yourself to experiment, pivot, and grow. Embrace the power of small consistent actions—they compound over time into big opportunities. This book is just the beginning. Keep revisiting your goals, stay curious, and surround yourself with people who inspire and challenge you. Use the tools, roadmaps, and strategies you've gained here as a launchpad to craft a meaningful, fulfilling career.

The future is waiting. Steer boldly toward it—one confident step at a time.

"Your career is your story. Make it worth telling."

YOUR CAREER COMPANION BEYOND THE BOOK

Your journey doesn't end with the final chapter — in fact, it's only just beginning. Steer was written to give you clarity, guidance, and momentum. Now, it's time to take action in the real world. We've created a digital extension of this book—designed to keep you updated, inspired, and connected long after you've closed the pages.

Scan the QR Code

- 1000+ Curated Job Profiles across Technology, Engineering, Healthcare, Business, and more
- Latest News & Updates on career trends, tools, and real-world opportunities
- Connect With Us for collaboration, guidance, or to bring career education to your school or organization

Your journey doesn't end with this book—this is just the beginning.

Contact ashhar@skillshark.in / +91-9028095540

Let's steer forward, together.